God's Faithful Ways

THE AUTOBIOGRAPHY OF NINFA P. PARSONS

God's Faithful Ways

© 2025 by Ninfa Parsons

All Rights Reserved

MASTER
P R E S S

All Scripture quotations are from:

King James Bible. (2017).
(Original work published 1769)

Printed in the United States

ISBN 978-0-9993750-7-5

For information:
MASTER PRESS
3405 ISLAND BAY WAY, KNOXVILLE, TN 37931

Mail to: publishing@masterpressbooks.com

FOREWORD

Ninfa Parsons is one of the most dedicated Christians I know. When my wife Leila and I first came to Trinity Community Church in Knoxville, Tennessee in July of 2011, we heard numerous stories about a passionate Filipina missionary. The members told us of the great wonders God had done through Ninfa. She was ministering in the southern part of the Philippines, her native home. Several in the congregation asked if my wife Leila was acquainted with Ninfa since she too was from the Philippines. Other than sharing a common national heritage, there had been no other connection up to that point. After several months of being with our new church family, Ninfa returned in 2012. We met her for the first time.

In the first few years of getting to know Ninfa, we witnessed that same passion we had heard about. Ninfa has a heart of compassion for the well-being of others, in physical needs as well as spiritual needs. She is always eager to share the great things the Lord has done in her ministry and thus bring glory to Christ. Ninfa is fervent in prayer, putting trust in God's Word above the circumstances which seem to declare the contrary. She is quick to repent and walks in humility.

I have the privilege to minister to Ninfa, minister with her and be ministered by her. The Lord uses Ninfa to speak things into my life, Leila's life, our Filipino Bible Study Group (FBSG) and many others here in Knoxville and globally. Ninfa is an intricate part of FBSG, launched in 2018. We refer to her as the matriarch. God has sovereignly woven together our ministries. She is a woman of great faith and zeal.

In 2013, Ninfa revealed to Leila and me the desire to record some of what the Lord had done in her life and ministry. She kept notes in a journal about the experiences she has had over the years, waiting for that open door the Lord was going to provide to make this vision come to life. In the latter part of 2020, I felt a stirring in my spirit to help Ninfa bring this God sent desire from a verbal commitment into a printed reality. Ninfa spent several hours with me in an interview style format as she reminisced about what great things the Lord has done for her and through her.

I have been enriched spiritually by hearing Ninfa's story. While helping her put together this autobiography, I have unearthed many amazing, untold events that the Lord has done throughout the course of her lifetime. Admittedly there were times when Ninfa had difficulty remembering the exact chronology of some of her life events, so some portions of the book are arranged topically instead of chronologically. It has been marked accordingly in various parts of the book to create more cohesiveness. We tried to follow the correct sequence of events as much as possible. That being said, all statements written therein, regardless of when they took place, are entirely factual. The fire in Ninfa's spirit for the things of God burns brighter than ever. History records many anointed women who served God passionately. Ninfa is one of them. She continues to impact countless lives just like Deborah the judge and Huldah the prophetess before her. I encourage everyone who names the Name of Christ to read this incredible journey of a faithful and zealous saint. As you read through these pages, you will be inspired!

—Garner Fritts, Ministry leader of FBSG Knoxville

ACKNOWLEDGMENTS

I thank God for my beloved parents who were so supportive and encouraging to me whenever I had problems and needs. I would also like to thank my daughters Edilyn Hall and Christine Bercero for supporting me and urging me to finish my autobiography in spite of all the busyness of life.

I would like to thank Garner Fritts for offering his assistance in interviewing, typing, initially editing, and acting as the liaison with the publisher so that I could finish the book and share it with the body of Christ. There had been so many delays in getting it done, and the Lord sent Him to me at just the right time to ensure that I crossed the finish line. I am thankful the Lord has brought him and his beautiful wife Leila into my life. They have been such a blessing to me.

I want to thank my FBSG Knoxville family. Without their financial sponsorship and encouragement in this project, it might not have been possible to have it distributed with a quality publication. I appreciate Barry Ehlers so much for his willingness to be a beta reader and manuscript reviewer. He and Loretta Ehlers have been part of my family for many years. I am very grateful for how they have shown me love and support in countless ways. I pray manifold blessings be upon you both. I want to give a big thank you to Maria Richardson for also reviewing the manuscript and bringing an additional literary critique to the book. It was very helpful. May the Lord greatly enrich you for your loving efforts. Thank you to Pastor Neil Silverberg and Master Press for taking on this book project and making its publication a reality. This also includes Patty King, the final editor who made this manuscript as clean and clear as possible. May God richly bless both of you.

I want to thank Rev. Arthur and Evelyn Thompson, the first missionary to Davao City in the Philippines from Los Angeles, California. They opened the Foursquare Gospel Church and the Halls of Life Bible College where I enrolled to learn more about God and how to serve Him in greater ways. Today, there are multiple Foursquare Gospel church locations in and around Davao City. They and the church were the inspiration the Lord used to propel me forward in ministry which led to the testimonies contained throughout this book.

Most importantly of all, I want to dedicate the book wholeheartedly to Jesus. To Him alone be all the glory! Great things He has done, and is still doing! I thank the Lord for His salvation, His love and His calling on my life. God has blessed me with wonderful friends, a beautiful family and a ministry in which I witnessed many miracles. At 84 years of age, I still feel the call of God to minister. I am grateful the Lord provided this opportunity to give testimony to the wonderful things He has done through the heart for ministry He gave me in the Philippines and America.

I also dedicate this book to all those who join with me in praising, thanking, magnifying and worshiping our faithful, miracle working God. I pray it is a blessing to everyone who reads it, and that it will inspire you to continue faithfully serving the Lord. I also pray that your faith will grow as I recount what amazing things God can do in someone's life when they surrender their hearts to His will. Jesus is the same yesterday, today and forevermore! (Hebrews 13:8) Hallelujah!

♦♦♦

1

HERITAGE OF THE LORD

Let me start with my early years. I was born on April 23rd, 1940 in Davao City, Philippines. It was a humble place far from the bustle of a major city. I came from a God-honoring home, raised by my loving parents Ramon Faustino Pizarro and Lourdes Rasmo Alba. I had two brothers and five sisters. My father managed a business that sold Singer sewing machines. Shortly after I was born, my parents dedicated me to God. Even though I was raised as a Christian, I was not sure of my salvation for quite some time. It was only my mother who was a true believer at first. My father had been an altar boy for the Catholic Church, but he had not experienced being born again. He had been raised in a devout, religious home. Mother Lourdes was attending the Baptist church at the time and did not try to convert my father. She just lived out her faith before him as the scriptures command (Matthew 5:16; 1 Corinthians 7:16). Ramon would not truly become a Christian until World War II took place.

My father grew very sick during World War II when the Japanese occupied the Philippines. As a young child, I saw my mother pray for his recovery and sing hymns over him. Mother Lourdes loved music. It touched my father's heart. Not only did he recover, he accepted Jesus into his heart as Lord and Savior and began to attend church with my mother. My parents became very active in church. Our family was a part of the United Church of Christ Philippines, or UCCP as we called it. Our denomination fell under the heading of Protestant. My father developed a great hunger for the Word of God. He continued growing in spiritual maturity. He became the head deacon, the head of the men's fellowship, and helped build the church facilities. My father was truly transformed!

When I was a little girl in Sunday School, the teacher who was over my age group taught us the song, My Home is in Heaven. It became the theme song for my class. I sang along but really did not understand what it was all about. When we finished the lessons, the teacher gave out candies. Though I wasn't sure about the things I was hearing concerning Jesus, I was happy to listen in order to get the treats. It was a very important lesson that I learned, and I would later implement the same strategies of treat distribution in my ministry. After several months of hearing the gospel, I began to have a hunger inside for the things of God. I continued to go to church with my parents for years as these feelings stirred more and more inside me.

There were many fearful encounters with the Japanese soldiers when they occupied the Philippines during World War II. When I was five years old, I remember walking with my parents and carrying around many household utensils. We had to flee at a moment's notice because of fighting in our villages. My mother had a simple coffee shop where the foreign soldiers would frequently stop to get a brewed cup and fried bananas.

There was a time when we had to evacuate our village to escape this fierce Japanese army. We carried as many belongings as we could as we ran into the forest. We were following a large group of our fellow villagers when we came across two different paths to take. Some of them wanted to go along one path while others with us wanted to choose the other route. A man appeared out of nowhere and encouraged us to follow him on the first path. He said it is the safest way. My family, along with some others from the village, followed his lead. It was the right choice, for we heard gunshots being fired in the distance. The others from our village who had spurned the advice of the stranger had been gunned down by the Japanese soldiers. We looked for that stranger to thank him, but he had vanished. We were convinced that it had been an angel from Heaven dispatched by God to ensure our safety. Once the war ended, we were able to resume somewhat of a normal life again.

I continued to grow in my faith as a teenager. I attended a Sunday School extension class in our neighborhood. There were only a few of us. The teacher continued to teach us Bible stories and songs. We also played many games and ate candy. Those sweets continued to be a big attraction for the children, including me. The teachers would ask us if we wanted to accept Jesus as our Savior so we could go to Heaven when we die. Everyone in the class, including me, raised our hands to the invitation and prayed along with our teacher. Something wonderful happened inside me that was hard to explain. It was at that moment that I knew Jesus had come into my heart. I felt like a new person. I was born again by the Spirit of God! (John 3:8). I was so happy. It wasn't long after this that our pastor water baptized me through immersion in a river in accordance to the commandment in the Bible (Acts 2:38). It was one of the greatest days in my life.

Every morning after my salvation experience, I started reading the Bible. I would read a chapter each day. Every time we went to church, I got very excited. I wanted to be a part of something my church was doing, so I joined the youth group. We had Bible study, prayer, games, and sharing of meals together. One day our youth leader encouraged us to do more beyond the confines of the church based activities. He said we need to go out and win other young people to Christ. We started splitting our youth group into teams and visited homes where young people resided. The Lord gave us boldness in our witnessing. One member of our group would share the message of salvation with people, and then we would all pray for the needs of those we met.

As our youth group grew larger and larger another wonderful thing happened. Some of the parents of these young people started coming to our meetings to see what it was all about. Our enthusiasm to serve the Lord was attracting the attention of many in the neighborhood. The parents noticed a positive change in the behavior of their youths. The Holy Spirit was transforming hearts all around us. The young people who joined us were suddenly respectful and motivated to do good works. A Bible study eventually began for the parents and grew just like the one for the youths. It was a wonderful testimony to what God was doing through us.

I remember a time when our youth group crossed a river in a small boat to hold Bible study with a family on the other side. While we were in the midst of the moving waters, we were suddenly hit by a strong wind. Such storms are common in the Philippines. The waves swelled to the point that it rocked the boat wildly. The others in the boat with me panicked and jumped out of the small boat because it was filling up with water. I stayed in because I could not swim. I sat there, praying hard that the Lord would stop this storm as I clutched the Bible against my chest. The storm subsided as quickly as it had come, and our boat did not sink. We finally made it to the shore. Everyone and everything was soaking wet, except for the Bible. The cover had a few water droplets on it, but none of the pages got wet or damaged. God had truly preserved His precious Word!

My parents and I continued to faithfully attend the Church of Christ, but eventually we heard about the Pentecostal Foursquare Church. We learned that they were praying for the sick and people were being miraculously healed. My baby sister Celedonia had been sick and had to be admitted to the hospital. She was seriously ill. A friend of mine and I became curious and decided to visit this church. It was led by the Reverend Arthur and Evelyn Thompson, a missionary couple originally from Los Angeles, California. We were amazed to see people so happy as they worshiped and praised the Lord. They clapped, lifted their hands heavenward and danced. The speaker that morning was a missionary who spoke like an angel. The topic that morning was healing. The church was a rented open-air building located just off the road where many people passed. It was easy for passersby to witness the meeting since the church was not hiding behind any walls. The service excited my spirit. When it was over, I went back home and pleaded with my mother to go to this new church. I told her that these Christians were praying for the sick. Since Celedonia was in the hospital, perhaps the Lord would heal her.

I found out that this church had a radio program, so my mother and I tuned in. The same missionary who had been speaking to the congregation that morning was on the air ministering. The topic, once again, was healing. As we listened, the missionary spoke a prophetic word stating that there was a sad family listening that very day with a seriously ill child in the hospital. Sometimes God supernaturally reveals something not known to a person in ministry. The minister will then declare it to those in need in order to incite faith in God and prepare the needy people to receive the answer to their prayers. That was what was happening with my mother and me. We knew that this Word was from the Lord, and it was for us. The voice from the radio told us to put our hands on the transistor as a point of contact. We did as this missionary had bidden us and we joined with her in prayer for my sister's miraculous restoration.

When my mother and I went to the hospital to see Celedonia, the doctor told us she was out of danger. In fact, she was getting better. We were so overjoyed with this news. Soon my sister was released from the hospital.

It wasn't long before my family decided to join the Pentecostal Foursquare Gospel Church and faithfully support it. Shortly after that, I got to know Evelyn Thompson better. She became a mentor and spiritual mother to me. She was an anointed woman of faith.

My family joined the Foursquare Pentecostal Church and faithfully supported it. My mother served as the head deaconess and leader of the women's ministry. She was very active in the women's fellowship. My mother was invited to other denominations to share her faith.

After my father retired, he took care of our small farm and

gave to our church's material needs. He donated equipment to the church, such as musical instruments, to further the ministry and outreach.

Sometime after that, however, my father became sick again and ended up in the hospital. His long-time friend Ariston Laurenta found out that my father was in the hospital. My father told Ariston that he had been thinking of him and longed to see him again. Even in his sickness, my father shared the gospel with his friend and led him to Christ. A few days after that, my father passed away. His friend Ariston would go on to serve the Lord faithfully and became active in church.

My father supported a pastor named Ike Zita. He was from a nearby village. At the end of each month, Ike would come to collect the support. After my father passed, Pastor Zita came to collect without knowing what had happened. My mother gave Ike the support that my father had promised. Pastor Zita came to the funeral home where my father was being kept before the burial. He was in shock over the death. Ike recalled how my father used to place gospel tracts in all the stores as a witness for Jesus. My father had a big heart to help the poor, and that heart carried over to me. My father was not a talker. He was a doer who loved to read Christian books. It is one of the reasons that compelled me to write this book about God's work in my life.

During my early years of ministry, my parents would often support me financially and came to places where I was ministering. They told me they were proud of how God was using my life. Though God had used me to minister to people many times already, I still struggled with fear and hesitation when it came to sharing my faith with people and ministering to them. I was usually one of the group members who prayed for others but was not out in front speaking. I wanted to be bold like the apostles were in the Book of Acts. (Acts 4:31) I was praying about all of this, asking the Lord to guide and give me the boldness I need to stand for Him. One night, God gave me a dream. Jesus wonderfully baptized me in the Holy Spirit and I spoke with other tongues. When I woke up it became a reality. The Lord suddenly replaced my shyness with a boldness that I could not explain. I no longer cared that someone would criticize me or think that I am strange for sharing my faith. It was a miracle for me, because it was not in my personality to be this way. I was a shy girl. The Lord was preparing me for a calling I would never forget.

◆◆◆

2

THE CALL FROM ON HIGH

After graduation from high school in 1959, I considered becoming a social worker or a nurse because I love people, especially the poor and the sick. Yet, I could not commit myself to follow that path. I was feeling a call within my heart to be in full-time ministry. There was a deepening hunger inside me to know God more and have an intimate relationship, not just know about Him. My zeal for ministry continued to grow.

Arthur and Evelyn Thompson were still meeting out in the open since they had yet to acquire a building. The missionary couple stood on a platform and led a gathering in teaching, songs and prayer. The attendees were not like typical Christians you might meet. There was such passion in their voices as they lifted up their praises to God. Fire burned in their hearts to serve the Lord every moment of every day and not just on Sunday. They genuinely enjoyed life and the Presence of Jesus. Evelyn was such an anointed woman of God! She gave an invitation for prayer with anyone who desired to serve the Lord with all their heart. I raised my hand and joined in this prayer.

After the meeting, I talked with Evelyn about the desires God had placed within my heart. She wanted to know where I wanted to serve in the body of Christ. I told her about my heart's desire to know God more intimately. That was my main goal above all else.

The Lord answered my prayer when Rev. Arthur and Evelyn Thompson launched the Halls of Life Bible College, or HLBC as we called it. I was one of the thirty students enrolled in the Bible College. The college was right in the center of Davao City, Philippines. Classes were Monday through Friday during the afternoon. I grew much deeper in the Word and the things of the Spirit during this time.

While studying for four years with HLBC, the other students and I were sent out to the streets to hand out gospel tracts and share the gospel. We often talked underneath trees, telling people how Jesus loves them and wants to bless them with His free gift of salvation. We always traveled in pairs when we were doing this work, for Jesus had sent out His disciples to proclaim His message by twos. (Mark 6:7) This was the preparation for us to learn how to start up new churches in various regions.

When I graduated from HLBC, my friend Josie Camacho and I were sent to help in pioneering a church in the small town of Malita, which is about three hours south of Davao City. In the beginning, we gathered children together, distributed treats, shared Bible stories with them, and taught them songs just like what I had experienced as a child. It began as an extension Bible school for children on the weekends. We also handed out gospel tracts to people we met. As we did this ministry, an amazing thing repeated just like what had happened years earlier. The parents were becoming interested in what we were teaching the kids, for they saw great changes in their behavior. It wasn't long before they joined us, and they became believers. We did not have a building yet. We gathered outdoors. Soon we were invited to have the meetings in the home of one of the parents.

We ministered in Malita for only a short time. I was summoned back after only a few months and traveled with the Thompsons to assist them in whatever church they were ministering. They sent another missionary to Malita to continue the work we started. After that, I moved to another church and continued the Lord's work there.

◆◆◆

3

ONWARD CHRISTIAN SOLDIER

My cousin Ninfa Alba and I were eventually called away to help elsewhere. Eugenio Galope pastored a church in Iloilo City. He asked my sending church for help. He had started several small churches on the island but could not oversee them all. They sent Ninfa Alba and I to help him handle this newly opened church. Pastor Galope took us by train to the town of Kalibo, Aklan. It is a city on the far north side of the island. It took several hours of travel time. Pastor Galope left us in the care of his Christian friends in Kalibo.

We stayed in this house for a short time while looking for a place to live and start ministering. After a few days, Ninfa Alba and I visited a nearby Baptist church. We were sitting in the back of the sanctuary. I was watching a family that sat close to the front of the church. I was just beginning to understand how the Holy Spirit was working in my life, but I heard an inner voice tell me that this couple was going to give us a place to stay. I was surprised by this inward impression. After the service, the members went around shaking hands in the usual manner of a typical congregation. We were introduced as missionaries from Davao City. The man God spoke to me about approached us. He introduced himself as Mr. Ibanes. He asked many questions of me and my cousin, one of which was about where we were living. We told the gentleman we haven't found a place yet because we had just come from Davao. Mr. Ibanes proceeded to tell us that he had a place for us to stay. This was my first of many revelations from the Lord, and it greatly encouraged me in the work that I felt He had called me to do.

The Ibanes family allowed Ninfa Alba and me to lodge in a room that was close to the kitchen area. We could look out the window and see the road. Though we had a place to stay, the Ibanes were not able to provide food for us. One evening, Ninfa Alba and I were very hungry. We had nothing to eat, but we trusted in our faithful Lord. Suddenly, we heard a knock on the door. When I opened it, a young Filipino stood there smiling. He was the Ibanes' family driver. In the Philippines, it is common to hire a family driver and pay them monthly. The driver drives the family car and stays with the family. He told us that he had rice and coffee for us. We were happy with this news, so we thanked God for His provision and ate until we were satisfied. We knew God would provide (Matthew 6:25-26).

Mr. and Mrs. Ibanes owned an insurance company. They had an office building that they worked from during the week. They offered it to us as a church meeting place on Sundays since they were closed on that day. We passed out tracts and invited people to the services.

As we continued ministering in Kalibo, we always started with children, for they are so open to hear the gospel stories. We fed them spiritually.

After a particularly hard day of ministry, Ninfa Alba and I returned to our room and experienced hunger pains once again. All we could afford to have was a Filipino biscuit cookie. We were thankful for that, but it wasn't enough to satisfy us. In the morning, we heard a commotion from the household helpers. They were fighting with helpers from another nearby household. In the Philippines, it is not uncommon for Filipinos to take in many helpers who cook, clean, and take care of domestic needs. In exchange, the helpers receive compensation like money for schooling and other needs. Just like other Eastern cultures, Filipinos have a community mindset.

I opened the window to see what all the fighting was about. The helpers of the Ibanes' neighbors were harvesting fish, and they were throwing it in anger. Some of the fish flying through the air made their way into our open window. It reminded me of the manna from heaven the Lord provided for the children of Israel in the wilderness (Exodus 16:4). We collected all of it and put it in a basket. I tried to give the fish back to the helpers, but they said they did not need it. They told us to keep it. It was bangus, a milkfish found in the local wet markets and the Philippines' national fish. A wet market is a public marketplace that sells fresh produce, meat and fish and other perishable goods in a non-supermarket setting. We were so happy to have bangus to eat. Ninfa Alba and I had wanted some ever since we saw it in the marketplace but we did not have the money. God once again provided for our needs and met the desires of my heart. When you delight in the Lord, He will do that (Psalms 37:4).

The Lord wasn't through caring for our personal needs. While we were grateful for the food that we had, I longed to eat some crab that I had noticed in the wet market. As usual, my cousin and I had no money. One day, after another busy time of ministry, we hurried home because it was raining hard. This is not uncommon in the Philippines. Several typhoons strike the country each year and bring with it high winds and floodwaters. It is the equivalent to the hurricanes in the Atlantic, except they are often fiercer. We are dependent on the heavy rains to make a healthy rice crop. By the time the morning came, our room had flooded. I slid out of my bed to go to the bathroom and saw something moving in the flowing waters. It was the crabs that I was craving to eat! Ninfa Alba and I collected the crabs. The Ibanes told us that whatever came into our room belonged to us. So we cooked the crabs and were satisfied again with our God-sent meal.

These are but a few of the many examples in which the Lord provided for our needs while we went about serving His purposes. We were learning to live by faith (Hebrews 10:38).

◆◆◆

4

GOING BACK HOME

I received a letter from my family telling me that my mother's right hand was infected and her eyes were hemorrhaging. Mother wanted to see me and to be with the whole family. Despite my mother's infirmity, she kept serving the Lord. She prayed all the time, read the Word through dim eyes and committed a lot of verses to memory. Mother was now in her sixties. Concerned she might pass away without us seeing each other again, I did not hesitate to take leave from Kalibo to be with her.

When I arrived, I felt so grieved at the sight. My mother was a diabetic, and gangrene had set up in her hands. The doctors were planning to amputate. In spite of her condition, she shared her faith with all the medical staff, visiting family members and anyone else who would listen.

My mother looked into my eyes and asked me if she could have a little bit of cake and ice cream. Of course that is not good for a diabetic, but the doctor said it would be okay if she had just a little bit. My mother's eyes brightened as she received this longed-for reward. She also asked me to pray for a miracle for her, which I gladly did and continued to do. When the doctors arrived to perform the surgery, they re-examined her hand. They said there was no longer a need for the operation. Her hand was improving. My brother and his wife stayed with mother that evening in the hospital. We didn't know it, but it would be her last night on this earth. My brother called me the next day with the news that our mother had gone home to be with Jesus. She received her complete healing in Heaven.

After my mother's passing, I was not able to return to Kalibo. My sending church dispatched another person to work with my cousin. I was assigned to pioneer another ministry in a village called Mudiang. It is just east of Davao City. While ministering there, I had a chance to attend a prophetic conference. The guest speaker paused in the middle of his sermon and pointed to me. He said he saw a vision of me being like a tree with many branches full of leaves. People were gathering underneath for shade from the heat of the sun. During the altar call, I went forward to be prayed for. When the visiting preacher stood in front of me, he prayed to confirm the Word that was spoken. I knew in my heart that this was a confirmation from the Lord as to how He planned to use me.

In another meeting inside one of our local auditoriums, a lady approached me and said that while we were praying together, she saw a vision of me standing before people sharing the Word of God. I was dressed in white and the congregation was also wearing white clothing. There were so many there listening, they filled the auditorium and spilled over to the outside. The words from this dear sister came true several months later. God had revealed more of His plan for my life

◆◆◆

5

MINISTRY LIFE PARTNER

During the first years of my missionary work, I was single. I continued my travels with the Thompsons, my American missionary friends, and assisted their ministry whenever I returned to my sending church. I would usually work with the young people. During an evangelistic campaign in the town of Tagum, I befriended a man named Marcelino Romero Tabin, my future husband. He was a loner who took things quite seriously. Marcelino and his family were not dedicated Christians initially even though they regularly attended church. He shared with me that he wanted to be a lawyer.

Something wonderful happened at the meetings in Tagum. When the preacher was calling people to come forward and accept Jesus as their personal Lord and Savior, Marcelino was among them. Marcelino was also filled with the Holy Spirit and became hungry for God. I overheard some of what he was telling one of the church workers afterward. He said that God was calling him into the ministry. At the end of the service, we went around shaking hands with everyone as we were accustomed to do. As I shook hands with Marcelino, I noticed that he was as interested in me as I was him. We became good friends. He and I met together every time the missionaries held meetings in our hometown. These evangelistic meetings motivated him to enroll at HBLC. That is where we really got acquainted with each other.

Marcelino eventually visited me in my hometown of Davao City. He stayed in the home of one of my Christian friends. This person was playing matchmaker. When Marcelino was introduced to this idea, he said he wanted to be like Paul and never marry. Yet he felt a fondness for me. As time passed, I felt that he wanted to be close to me, yet I was not attracted to him at that time. As I got to know Marcelino more, I was drawn to his spiritual life. It was then that I fell in love.

While Marcelino was in the Bible College, he tried to court me. I initially told him I was not interested in that kind of commitment, for my only desire was to serve the Lord. He didn't take that as a final answer. Marcelino proposed and kissed me on the cheek. Filipinos are usually shy about such things. I was taught not to display too much affection if you are unmarried. Though I did not show it, I was excited by what happened. I finally agreed to his advances and we were engaged to be married.

After Marcelino graduated from Bible College, he was assigned to pastor a church in Kiamba, Cotabato. It was about a five-hour drive from Davao City. I was assigned to minister in the village of Mudiang, which was close to Davao City. We did not have much communication. It took more than a month to receive Marcelino's letters. He lived so far away from where I was, maintaining a relationship was hard. Because of a lack of communication and the inability to make a real commitment to each other, I called off the engagement.

During this time, I went with a team from our sending church to minister to a church that gathered in a public compound on the property of a rich widow. It was in Ilang Tibungco, which is in the Bunawan district of Davao City. Many people frequently used the compound for parties and other events. We were allowed to conduct meetings in that place. While I was sharing my faith in Jesus, the rich widow came out to listen. She was angered by what I was saying, so she got a rifle to threaten me. Her son, Tony Babao, rescued me by stepping between us and stopping his mother from using the rifle on me. After she settled down, I invited people in prayer to accept Jesus. Tony came forward and gave his heart to the Lord. His mother watched in silence and never said anything about it.

The following evening, Tony came to my parsonage and serenaded me. He called out to me and said that after he received Jesus, he was too excited to sleep. Tony told me that he kept seeing me in his dreams. I told him that it must be Jesus speaking to his heart. Mr. Babao thought he was in love with me, but I told him he must first be in love with Jesus.

Day after day, Tony kept coming to my parsonage, serenading me and bringing me gifts. He said he became a Christian and told me that he wants to marry me. I told Tony that I had already been engaged. He still tried to win me. Tony said that even if someone is about to eat a certain food, sometimes it falls from our hands and is lost before the first bite. I was double-minded and entertained the possibility of being with this man. Part of me wanted to marry someone with money and good looks. Tony Babao had both.

I went to my knees and prayed about it. I needed confirmation. I could not get peace about being with Tony. I knew the Lord's will is often confirmed by a sense of inner peace about a situation (Philippians 4:7). A visiting minister had asked me if I was married. I told him about my previous relationship with Marcelino and my current thoughts about Tony. I thought perhaps I could be with Tony. The minister asked to see pictures of Marcelino and Tony, which I had with me. After looking them over, he prayed and the Lord showed him that Marcelino was the man that God wanted me to marry. He also said that we would be ministering together. This was the confirmation I needed.

I resumed writing letters to Marcelino. He had also written to me asking for our relationship to be restored. I went back to Davao City and he met me at the airport. Not too long after that, we were married.

After our wedding, Tony watched us from afar and kept getting drunk in sorrow over losing me. I told him that if he truly had Jesus in his heart as he had previously stated, then he should act like it and stop getting drunk. Years passed by. He died in a car accident, but did come back to God before dying.

Marcelino and I served faithfully in whatever the ministry leaders of the Pentecostal association of the Philippines asked us to do. After we were married, he was transferred back to Davao City. Our first church together was in Toril. It was only a one hour drive from the city and close to the sea. We did not pioneer very long. Our denomination called us back to Davao City again where I taught in the Bible School on the subjects of the Holy Spirit and Evangelism. Marcelino was assigned to take care of the Children's church. We were also asked to be the managers of the Bible school dormitory.

Marcelino and I eventually became parents. He was the father of my four children, two handsome sons, and two beautiful daughters. Junemar, or Bong, was the eldest. He was born on June 25, 1966. Raphael, or Jojo as we called him, was the second child. He was born May 3, 1968. Edilyn was the third child. She was born December 18, 1971. The baby of the family, Christine, was born December 21, 1973.

After only a few years of serving together, we received the news that my husband had developed colon cancer. We discovered it because of the stomach pains he had been experiencing. The report discouraged me. I watched him get sicker and sicker. The time came when he was no longer able to work by my side. Marcelino ended up being admitted to the hospital and stayed there for a long time. I visited with him every chance I got. One of the nurses told me that Marcelino needed some medications and a blood transfusion. I was worried because I didn't have the money to buy things. As I sat near the nurses' station praying about it, a man approached me. I recognized him. He was the driver of one of my good friends. He said he had been looking for me. He pulled an envelope out of his pocket and placed it in my hands. I asked him who was giving this to me. He said that the person who did so wanted to remain anonymous. I presumed it came from my friend whom he worked for, but he was told to tell me that it was from the Lord. Inside the envelope was the exact amount of money I needed for all the medical care that Marcelino needed! Even in the midst of our trials, God was proving to be a faithful Caregiver to His sons and daughters just like He did for Elijah the prophet! (1 Kings 7:1-7).

I traveled many times to and from the hospital to check on my husband. Our kids were still small and we prayed frequently for the Lord's provision during this difficulty. God put it on the hearts of neighbors and others to supply food as we dealt with this issue. Sometimes we ate only rice mixed with soy sauce, but we were grateful for everything we had.

The treatments Marcelino received managed his medical condition, but it did not stop its progression. My husband had been writing a book titled Attitude. He had to stop working on it and would never finish it. I prayed for his healing and for the strength to bear this burden. The answer I longed for did not happen. Within a year of the cancer diagnosis, Marcelino passed into the Presence of the Lord. We had been married for ten wonderful years.

This was a practical and hard lesson that it is God's will, not ours. I prayed fervently for my husband's healing. I had seen many that were healed by God, but not my husband. There is no explanation for when, where, why, and how God heals some and not others. I understood that God's ways are often mysterious (Deuteronomy 29:29), and at the same time, He is a great Healer (Exodus 15:26). I also knew that Jesus was faithful, and all things would eventually work together for the good of His servants who are called according to God's purposes (Romans 8:28).

◆◆◆

6

THE WIDOW'S DIVINE PROVIDER

There was a convention going on in Davao City at the time of my husband's death. Some of the missionaries in the area helped us with the funeral proceedings. The preacher delivered the message while family and friends gathered around the casket. Afterwards, the missionary wanted to pray for the hurting loved ones. Once the prayer had ended, this lady said she saw a vision of smoke coming from Marcelino's coffin. She watched it rest on top of my head. The smoke had taken the form of Marcelino's face. She believed it was the mantle of my husband's anointing passing on to me, similarly to how the anointing passed from Elijah to Elisha when Elijah was taken to Heaven (2 Kings 2:9-15).

I continued to take care of the Bible school without my life partner. I remained a widow for ten years, raising my children in the fear of the Lord as I tried to continue in the ministry God had given me. I worked with youth programs through our church affiliation. I also became the director of the women's ministry in various places around Mindanao. It is the northwestern part of the island and about a ten-hour car ride away from Davao City. My young children would stay with my sister Cornelia while I traveled to different places serving the body of Christ. The only time I recall my kids coming with me is when my youngest daughter Christine came along while I taught and had intercession with my prayer group. She took pictures of me ministering in the village. She would then lie on the floor and sleep until I finished.

I wondered how I could move forward in the work of God without my life partner by my side. I knew things would become harder, but the Lord promised in His Word to give grace and help in times of need (Hebrews 4:16). Before he died, Marcelino prophesied to me that God would not only use me in the denomination we had been working in, but also many other denominations. This divine prediction came true as I would eventually work with the Missionary Alliance, Baptists, Catholics, and many other groups. The doors would open wide for me, and I realized I could never have done any of this on my own. It was the Lord's doing, for it is all about Him.

I wasn't finished working within my denomination, but many invitations came to speak with other church groups. They wanted to know more about the ministry of the Holy Spirit. There was a hunger in the hearts of people. I still had good fellowship with the Pentecostal Foursquare Church I was connected to, but I was not as active with them at that time. They were expecting me to bring the newly Spirit-filled believers into their particular denomination and out of the ones they had previously been a part of. This did not happen, for I felt it was more effective just doing it in the way that I had been accustomed. I did not know it at the time, but these connections to other church groups would be the means by which I would eventually get to come to the United States of America. I would never break ties with my former church. I was eternally grateful in how the Lord used them to teach me the ways of God and the power of the Holy Spirit.

The Lord opened up many and varied opportunities to share the gospel with those in governmental places. The chief of the local police in Davao City was not happy with me when he discovered that his wife became a Christian. They had a sick child that I prayed for. When the baby recovered the following day, the chief learned that I had prayed for their child's healing. He told me that this faith I had must be real. He got saved and opened up his house for Bible studies and prayer meetings. The chief also invited me to his precinct and allowed me as much time as I needed to speak to all of the officers. The Lord moved mightily in their midst.

The Lord also used me to reach out to men and women in the military. A ministry friend named Pol Roma invited me to his church in Manila to minister for a few months. He also brought me to different Bible studies. I met a general named Saavedra who was in charge of the Philippine military. I found out that he was a relative on my father's side and a Christian. Gen. Saaverda asked me to come to the military headquarters to share the gospel.

The Lord used me to reach into some remote villages. I visited a family in a village that you had to cross a river to reach it. They were quite hospitable to me, but not all of them. The wife of the family introduced me to her brother Panfilo Villa Abrielle. He was visiting from another village. He wanted to meet me and inquire about my ministry. After our prayer time together,

Panfilo approached me and said he had questions for me about my Bible teachings. His sister said that he wanted to debate with me. I told them that I believed in the Lord and the Bible. That was the truth and that is what is needed. I spoke to Panfilo about my experience and about salvation. I told him that I served Jesus because I was happy to know Him and so glad I was on my way to Heaven. I asked Panfilo if he wanted assurance that he was saved and on his way to Heaven, but he became quiet.

After two or three weeks, Panfilo came to visit his sister and told her he wanted to meet with me again. He had more questions, but not like before. Panfilo said that he had not experienced the salvation I was talking about and wanted it in his life. The Spirit of God had begun to change his heart. When I finally met him again, he invited me to come and speak to his Bible study group. I was happy to do so. Some ministry friends of mine came with me to his village. We had to cross the river again in order to get there. When we arrived, the Spirit of the Lord stirred this Bible study group. All of them were born again! Panfilo ended up going to Bible college and becoming a pastor. He even started new churches in that village! Though I have not seen Panfilo in years, I hear that God was doing great things in their midst.

Around this time, I had grown cold in my heart even though I continued to go through the motions of ministry. My relationship with the Lord had suffered while I was in this backslidden state. I wasn't very effective in the things I was doing. During my time of inner struggle, a British missionary named Edith Watson visited the area. She was a single lady who had previously been in nursing. She stayed in California prior to coming to the Philippines. Edith was going house to house in Davao, handing out gospel tracts and praying with people. She came to my home and handed me one of these tracts. I told her I was a graduate of the local Bible School.

Edith invited me to join her in visitation. I perceived that God was drawing me back into His mission again. I observed how friendly Edith was with the natives. You could see the love of Jesus in her demeanor and presentation. It was a stark contrast to the spiritual condition I was in. I was still struggling with coldness and frustrations in my heart. I was dealing with anger and bitterness, yet I would continue to go through the motions of church life. She was led by the Lord to ask me to go with her to minister and spread the gospel. She planned to minister to villages that did not speak English. In order to succeed, she needed an interpreter. The Lord touched my heart to go with her. In one of the services, Edith called people forward to renew their commitment to Jesus. She was surprised that I was the first one to come and be prayed for. God had warmed my heart and restored the passion in my spirit for Him and His work.

I traveled with Edith and served as her interpreter. Although English is the second language of the Filipinos, there are some who have never ventured outside the country or are uneducated and know very little of it. Tagalog is the official national language and there are numerous regional and local dialects spoken. To have a far-reaching impact in these places, knowing the language or having an interpreter is very important. Edith needed me to translate her English into Visayan, my regional dialect.

We went into the town of Cotabato. It was a Muslim village. We had to take a boat to reach the churches on this island. We lodged in a small parsonage near the seashore. The pastor of one of these churches told us of an amazing incident that happened just before we arrived. He saw several small boats approaching along the seashore. Some Filipino rebels had been active recently in their place. The villagers were afraid of what this might be. It had become dangerous for the natives to walk around their own neighborhoods. The pastor had heard of some people being harassed or even killed. These boats carried Filipino pirates looking to plunder the seaside villages and make trouble for Christians. A man who had been part of the rebels recounted the event to the pastor. He deserted them after what he had witnessed. He said that as he and his fellow pirates neared the seashore, they saw several tall men standing along the shore in white apparel. They were holding swords. The pirates were terrified, so they fled and didn't return. We recognized this as another miracle from God to clear the way for us to minister freely in this village.

While we were there, I received news that my ten-year-old niece Priscilla had died due to a heart condition. I wanted to go back to Davao City and be with my family, but there was no transportation available. The buses and the roads had been closed because of the rebel activity in the area. It saddened me, but I knew God would be with my family just as He was with me. The pastor told Edith and me that a small private plane just landed in their town. They were planning to fly us back to Davao City that day. The pilot offered to give us a ride back to the city if we wanted it. God had provided a way for me to go back home and be with my grieving family.

Edith and I would continue visiting all types of denominations outside the Pentecostal circles, including Catholic ones. There were many different types of believers from varied independent affiliations. We encouraged pastors, trained more church workers, and prayed with many people. Some of the ones to whom we ministered, left their churches to begin new ones which moved in the charismatic gifts of the Holy Ghost. Soon after this, I got involved with more missionaries coming into my area and the ministry expanded further. It was a beautiful time of service in which the Spirit was moving in supernatural power.

While Marcelino was alive, we lived off of the income he earned from the insurance business. Without my husband, I had the challenge of providing for the needs of my young children while trying to be faithful to God's calling. Yet I never forgot that God was my Jehovah Jireh, which means the Lord will provide. He proved His great care for me time and time again.

There was a time I had left a village after ministering, and I realized I had no money to buy food for my family. I had gone to the church with only twenty pesos in my pocket. (Approximately fifty pesos is the equivalent to one American dollar at that time). I had every intention of feeding my kids with this money. I was hesitant to put it in the offering because of our need, but the Holy Spirit was prompting me to give it away. God reminded me that He has always provided for me, so He would do so even now (Philippians 4:19). I asked the Lord to forgive me for doubting Him, and I would willingly and graciously give my twenty pesos to His work.

One day at my sending church, my daughter Edilyn came running to me and said there was someone downstairs of the church who wanted to see me. He had a big box full of dressed chicken in plastic bags. I told Edilyn to get the boxes and put them in the refrigerator. It turned out that the man was the driver of one of my wealthy church friends. She had recently accepted Jesus as her Savior. Her freezer had broken, so they had to take all of it out. They didn't want it to spoil and did not have any place else to store it. They needed to give it away. The first thing that came to my friend's mind was to give all of it to me.

When I took the boxes of chicken home, I could not fit them into my small refrigerator. I distributed the extra chicken to my neighbors and to the ministers that lived nearby. That evening at the church, I was surprised to see my neighbors in the service. They were not believers. They approached me afterwards and wanted to know why I had given chicken to them and asked where it came from. I shared my testimony about giving my last twenty pesos in the offering and how the Lord provided for the needs of my family. I wanted to share my blessing with them. They told me that this act of kind generosity moved them so much, they wanted to visit my church. They shared this testimony with the congregation and soon became a part of us. So Jesus not only provided for my needs, but He gave more chickens to share with my neighbors, providing for the physical and eventually spiritual needs of those around me. He really is a good God!

Around this time, I befriended a lady nurse named Dinah Edijer. She was the director at Exodus Community Health Center. She founded this clinic with help from the government and volunteer medical staff. Their main objective was to help poor people who could not afford proper care. She was involved with several churches. I partnered with Dinah in this ministry. She was trying to establish a spiritual development program, and she asked me to coordinate that with her. Whenever they reached the limits medically with a patient, they sent them to the spiritual department where I would pray for their needs. Dinah and I gathered often to pray for the ministry and for other prayer requests from people. I started a Bible study in that clinic with the doctors and nurses.

Dinah would often stay in my house. She watched over my four kids when I had ministry appointments and one day she took Christine with her to the clinic. Dinah was very generous. She gave a lot to help people. Dinah was suspected of being an activist for political rebels because of her extravagant generosity toward them and other poor people in the community. The Filipino police had Dinah under surveillance and brought her to the local precinct to be investigated. Christine had to accompany Dinah to the police station since she was only six years old and could not be left there with anyone else. I had to get Christine because Dinah would be imprisoned for almost a year. Dinah was placed in the women's section of the jail. She befriended all the policemen and prisoners. I often visited her. She witnessed to everyone she could in the prison. Dinah organized a prison church where many people accepted the Lord. I helped Dinah whenever I could while she was incarcerated. The prisoners prayed Dinah would not be released so she could keep doing the Lord's work there. The staff at Exodus Community Clinic continued the work in the center while Dinah remained in custody. She was finally released and resumed her duties at the center.

The time came when I was once again in need of necessities. There was literally nothing in the refrigerator to feed my family, and I had no money to buy anything. I had learned that God was my Jehovah Jireh (Genesis 22:14), so I placed my hands on the refrigerator and prayed that the Lord would fill it with food for my family. My friend Dinah visited that day and joined me in this petition. Dinah suddenly stopped praying and started laughing. She told me she was seeing a vision of a big can of Nido powdered milk. This is a brand that we carry in the Philippines. I had not told Dinah that I ran out of milk and was in need of more. All of a sudden, there was a knock at the door. When I opened it, I saw a friend of mine named Cora Tuason standing at the threshold. She told me that while she was shopping at the market, the Lord spoke to her heart to buy us groceries. Cora entered my home and filled my refrigerator with a box full of food! She had also brought us a big can of Nido powdered milk!

Cora had been a devoted Catholic friend of mine. She had once asked me to pray for her because she had a lot of checks coming in that were bad. It was hurting them financially. A few weeks later, she came back to me excited. Many good checks had come in and supplied their needs. She became more interested with what the Lord was doing in my ministry. Her family opened their homes for Bible studies, fellowship and prayer meetings. One of Cora's priests came and attended our fellowship. He was very interested in what the Lord was doing among us. The priest invited me to speak in their church and share the gospel. From that time on, some of them became regular attendees to our fellowship. Cora started serving the Lord and took some of her friends to Muslim villages and helped needy pastors build their churches. Her Filipino husband eventually passed away and she married an American. She is still working for Jesus to this day.

As my children grew older, I had to send them to school. The Philippines required tuition fees that had to be met in order for kids to attend school. Without that, they wouldn't receive an education. I remember one particular time that I needed additional funds for Bong and Jojo to continue their studies. I once again went to my knees to petition the Lord for provision. While I was praying, there was a knock at my door. I thought God was about to answer my prayer right then and there. I opened the door and saw a woman standing there with her hand out, palm upward. This lady helped me part-time because she needed money to buy food for her children. I asked her to wait since I didn't have the money yet to pay her. She was okay with that for the moment. I resumed praying even though I was worried. I told the Lord that I trusted Him and I was sure He would provide.

There was a second knock on my door. It was another Christian friend of mine who dropped by to visit. She said she had been at home praying when the Lord impressed me and my children in her heart. She pulled out a handful of money and placed it in my hands. It was the exact amount I needed for the helper and for the tuition of my two boys!

When Christmas came to the Philippines, I wondered how I could treat my children with gifts. They were asking for presents. I told them that the Lord will supply all that we need. We prayed together every night as the holiday approached. On Christmas morning, my children and I came downstairs to find a lot of food and gifts for us. Someone from another church was impressed by God to deliver this to us. We had a happy and blessed Christmas miracle that year.

I recall a time when I had the chance to be a blessing. I had an inner prompting to take some bananas that had been sitting on my table to an American missionary serving for a year in my area. Her name was Darlene Sizemore. The Philippines have smaller bananas in a variety of colors. When I went to her house with the fruit in hand, she couldn't contain her joy. Darlene told me that she had been craving Filipino bananas and was hoping to have some. I perceived this as the Lord supplying the desires of her heart as she worked faithfully for Him. There is no request too big or too small for our God!

In every circumstance, I realized that if Jesus has called you, then He will faithfully supply everything you need to ensure that His will is carried out. We are blessed to be a blessing!

———

7

CONFLICTS IN THE CAMP

Being like Jesus while serving in the ministry has not always been easy. Some of the hardest things to handle weren't with unbelievers, but with my own brothers and sisters in Christ.

I remember when my young son was playing with one of the other boys in our church. Suddenly, they started fighting. The mother of the other child came on the scene to see what was happening. She was one of my fellow ministry partners. What's more, she was also my close neighbor. I looked on as she tried to slap my son. I became angry and told her she should not have done that. Hatred took root in my heart for this woman. Ironically, she was a part of a conference that was teaching about the love of God. As she shared that message with the group, I could not stop thinking about her angry attitude and putting her hands on my son.

I felt awful and defeated thereafter. Ministry was a struggle. Anytime I saw my neighbor out and about, we would avoid each other by walking a different route. The Holy Spirit convicted me and prompted me to forgive her. I told the Lord it was hard to love her. What she did was not Christ-like. I finally gave in and asked God to help me forgive her. The next time I saw her along the way, I did not avoid her like I did before. Amazingly enough, neither did she. The Spirit was about to do a work of reconciliation in my heart. As we crossed paths, I reached out and hugged her. I told her that I loved her.

I immediately felt a burden unload from my spirit. Joy and peace that I had not experienced in a while flooded my soul. She embraced me tightly and began to weep. We forgave one another then and there, and she and I have had a good relationship ever since.

My sending church had wanted me to bring the newly Spirit-filled people I had ministered to from the other denominations into the Pentecostal Foursquare Church. I did not believe it should be done, and they had threatened to take my ministry license. Eventually, the tension between me and the Pentecostal Foursquare Church was finally resolved. Perhaps they recognized it was just part of the charismatic movement that was sweeping across the world. Many people from all kinds of denominations were being baptized in the Spirit and were operating in the gifts of the Spirit. They too, remained in their respective churches. It was a move of God that I was privileged to be a part of.

These events showed me that the children of God will

undoubtedly face conflicts within the body of Christ. I've come to realize that as you become farther along in your walk with Jesus, you will learn to be a peacemaker and turn things over to the Lord, for He will resolve our disputes (Romans 12:17-21).

◆◆◆

8

THE WIDOW'S DIVINE PROTECTOR

God has always protected me, throughout my life. In doing His work, I would oftentimes find myself in difficult circumstances. But the Lord protected me and rescued me from all harm (Psalms 91:1-16). Many times He put things in motion before I knew I needed the help. Here are some examples:

On one occasion, I attended an all-night prayer vigil that was close to the market. Several people came and remained until it was over, but I was not able to stay the entire time. I approached the road side to see if I could still find anyone around who could take me back home. I was praying for provision and protection. It was so late that all the public transportation was finished until the following morning.

In the distance, I saw two men walking down the street coming toward me. I was feeling uneasy about this, especially since I was alone. As the two men got close, a taxi pulled up out of nowhere. He opened the door and motioned for me to quickly get inside. As the driver sped off, he told me that those men were bad people. He felt compelled to come out there, and now he knew why. The Lord protected me from danger. I was never happier to be at home, finding peace there and in my heart.

On another occasion, I became close friends with a helpful family who had money. Although I recall their names, I will not disclose it, for it might put them in danger even now if I do so. The wife was a recent convert of the ministry. She often visited when I was ministering in Bible studies. Their daughter was also one of my good friends. The daughter told me that her mother and father would often go out and enjoy various activities. Robbers knew about their wealth and threatened them on many occasions. They would pacify the thieves' demands or run away. When some other troublemakers in the area figured out that this family had money, they sent the mother a letter asking for some of it. They issued threats in an attempt to commit extortion. These thieves said they would do harm if their demands were not met. They also threatened to hurt this family if my friend's mother contacted the police.

I was visiting at the time they received the letter. They were afraid to leave their home, but I had to go so I could feed my kids and do some errands. Once we finished our fellowship, I bid the family farewell and signaled for a jeepney to take me back home. I was not aware at first, but these agitators who had threatened my friends were following me. I had actually seen these men before in one of my meetings. At one of the stopovers, I had to mail a letter at a nearby post office.

When I crossed the street, I noticed that those men had been watching and were coming toward me. There were three of them. They were friendly to me, asking where they could get some parts for their car. They claimed it had broken down and they needed some help. I told them that the stores were only a few blocks away. They asked me to guide them to these places.

Being a single woman who was all alone in this situation, I felt very uneasy in my spirit. The Lord spoke to my heart and let me know that I was in danger. Another man stood next to a car parked only a few meters away. The guy closest to me signaled for him to come and join them. I was certain that they were about to kidnap me. I figured they were going to try to ransom me to the family they threatened since they knew I was friends with them.

I closed my eyes and started praying in the Spirit. The sweet Presence of the Lord surrounded me. When I opened my eyes, I was inside the Post Office! It was a similar experience to what happened to Philip the evangelist when he was transported from one place to another by the Holy Spirit. (Acts 8:39-40) The men outside were searching everywhere for me. When they saw me standing in the post office, they beckoned for me to come to them, but I refused. I told them that they should come to me, for there was a crowd inside the building, including a security guard.

Eventually, they left and nothing happened, for the Lord rescued me from danger on that day. I went to the police station and reported the incident. They got involved, the men disappeared and my blessed friends never heard from them again.

This was not the only time God provided deliverance for me and my Christian friends. Another family whom I led to the Lord had invited me to hold Bible studies in their house. They had teenage children and maids living with them. We had been studying about the baptism of the Holy Spirit and the gifts of the Spirit. They all became hungry to receive from God everything that was available to them. I told them God will fight against our enemies and empower us to do the work He has called us to. The family and all their helpers were filled with the Spirit.

One day when I was at home taking care of some business, I received a phone call from the mother of this family. She told me they had received a letter from the NPA (New People's Army) faction. This political group is the armed wing of the Communist Party of the Philippines seeking democratic revolution. They usually reside in the countryside, especially the mountains. The letter indicated that the rebels wanted some food and money to sustain them. They would be dropping by to collect it. Many Filipinos are afraid of this group and try to avoid them as much as possible.

The wife asked if I would come to their place and help them pray against this uncomfortable request. I told her that I would pray for her and the family, but I was unable to come at that particular time. I gave her instructions to pass on to the family. I felt that it was the Voice of the Lord telling me to do so. I told her that when the rebels come to their house, they just need to ask God for wisdom and guidance in what to do. I told them to recite the Lord's Prayer as well, for we had memorized it in our Bible study time.

Late that evening, the NPA was at their door knocking. When they opened the door for the rebels, they began to pray loudly, recite the Lord's Prayer, lift their hands and worship Jesus. The soldiers suddenly fell under conviction and dropped the guns they were holding. They lifted their hands and joined in reciting the Lord's Prayer. When the vigil ceased, the men told this family that they had been asked to impose these demands because their faction had run into some hardships. They explained that they are not really bad people, but they were very hungry and in need. The rebels asked them not to be afraid and pleaded for assistance of some kind.

This opportunity created an opening to share the gospel. The family witnessed to these men about Jesus and invited them to join in their weekly Bible study. The next time I visited to conduct the Bible study, the soldiers were there. They wanted to keep a low profile though, for they were concerned that getting caught doing this would get them into trouble with their faction.

The Lord is a mighty defense from all harm (Psalms 5:11-12). Praise His holy Name!

◆◆◆

9

EVERY FILIPINO'S DREAM

I'll never forget the excitement I felt when I found out that my friend Rachel and I would have the chance to go to the United States of America. For many Filipinos, going to America is a dream come true. There was a Bible camp meeting going on in Ashland, Virginia. Each year there was an international camp where ministries from different countries went to receive teaching from the Lord about such things as encouragement, guidance, empowerment and other ministry enriching blessings. There was free food and lodging. I felt led by God to take part. All I had to do was pay for transportation.

Though I had no money for the plane ticket, I felt that the Lord wanted me to go to this camp meeting. I not only needed the funds for this trip, but I also needed the funds to secure the nourishment of my children in my absence. So by faith, I started packing. I had to go to Manila, the capital city of the Philippines, to be interviewed for a passport and visa in order to leave the country. The Philippines is divided into three main regions, which are Luzon in the north (where Manila is the capital city), Visayas in the middle, and Mindanao in the south (where my hometown of Davao City is located). Our country is made up of thousands of islands, and the only way to reach many of them is by boat or plane. I would wait on the Lord again to see what He would do.

The next morning, Rachel dropped by with some mixed news. The bad news was, something had come up and she would not be able to go. The good news was, she already had the money for the airfare, and she wanted me to have it. I went to Manila with my friend and four other ladies. The other women told me that they had rough interviews with the immigration officers. They were told that they should have money in their accounts, own properties in the Philippines, and that their trip to the United States could only be very short. One of the reasons for such strict policies about visiting America had to do with the number of people who made the trip and never returned. The Filipino government tried to prevent that from happening. It was especially hard for single women to travel to the United States since it was common for many Filipinas to marry American men.

I knew God had not brought me this far to be stopped now. Even though I met none of the requirements set forth by immigration, I believed by faith that the Lord would work this out for me and provide, somehow. I fell into a line where I saw many Filipinos walk away with sad looks on their faces. They had been turned down for a chance to visit the United States. They were telling those of us in line that the man who was interviewing them was very strict.

I prayed silently in the Spirit. When I came face to face with the officer, he spoke very kindly to me. Everyone around me was so surprised. He never asked me about any bank accounts I possessed. He never mentioned anything about properties I owned. The only thing he wanted to know was what my intentions were in going to Ashland, Virginia. I told him that I wanted to attend an international camp meeting for religious purposes. I also told him that I wanted to know more about God. He inquired if I had children, to which I answered in the affirmative. After a moment, he told me that I would have my visa and passport the following week.

My sister Cornelia graciously provided me with extra money to travel to Virginia and attend the camp. When I went to the agency to get my plane ticket, I was told that the flights were fully booked and there were no more open seats for me. The next thing available would be well past the time of the camp meeting. I was not discouraged though. I prayed and told Jesus that He had opened the door for me several times already, and I needed Him to do it again. I stayed overnight in the place where I had been interviewed, and the next morning I was preparing to go back home. Just before I left, the travel agent who had turned me down the previous day stopped me. She said the agency contacted her and said a seat became vacant. A passenger had suddenly decided to give up his spot. It wasn't long until I boarded the plane and took my first flight to America. Praise God!

Our first stop was in California. I visited one of the towns where my sister lived. She married a Filipino pastor who was ministering to a Filipino church in the area. When I told them why

I had come to America, they told me it was a three-day journey by bus to reach my destination. I didn't know the geography of America yet, so I had no idea how far Virginia was from the west coast. That evening, I attended their Bible study. I had trouble staying awake because of the time zone difference and jet lag. I was asked to testify about the ministry in the Philippines. When the meeting was over, my sister's husband said they do not normally take up an offering during the Bible study, but he felt compelled by the Holy Spirit to do it and give me the money. What they had given was the exact amount that I needed to pay for a bus ticket to the other side of the country! Before I left, some of the church people slipped cash into my pockets and told me it was for snacks along the way.

When I reached Ashland, Virginia, I remained on the campgrounds for a month. There were intense prayers during the meetings and the gifts of the Spirit were in full operation among these ministry leaders. I learned about exercising the gifts of the Spirit. They asked me to share my testimony about the Philippine ministry, which I am always eager to do. It was a powerful experience that I will never forget. The Lord was opening more doors for me to serve Him.

At the closing of the camp meeting, some pastors invited me to testify in their churches concerning the work in the Philippines. I had the opportunity to visit more than ten states to share my testimony. Every time I ran out of money, the Lord touched the heart of someone to give me lodging and transportation in every place of which I was asked to come. Another time, while I was in California, a friend of mine gave me the name of a man who needed a pen pal. His name was Glen Parsons. For those who were born in the 20th century, this is how we used to communicate long distance. We would write long letters to friends, mail them and wait several weeks to get a response. They told me that Glen also loved God dearly and wanted to be involved in ministry. So, we began regularly writing to each other.

During my prolonged stay in California, Glen started calling me from Texas. He was from Knoxville, Tennessee but was visiting his brother in Houston. It wasn't long before he came to see me. We got married shortly thereafter in California. A few days after our wedding, we flew to Houston, Texas, got into Glen's car, and drove into Knoxville. Glen took me to his home church called Trinity Chapel. He introduced me as his new bride to Steve Fatow, the pastor of the church. He told him that I was a missionary. Trinity Chapel, and Knoxville, Tennessee, would become my second home when I was away from the Philippines.

I returned to Los Angeles to prepare and return to the Philippines to see my children again. Edilyn had requested that I get a doll for her ever since I first arrived in America. Not wanting to disappoint my precious little girl, I searched far and wide for the toy she wanted, hoping that I would find it and that the money for it would be available. I stayed with one of my friends, named Gloria, before taking the long flight back to my home in the Philippines. Gloria shared that she was having trouble in her marriage, and she wished to be filled with the Holy Spirit. I prayed for her before I left, and God wonderfully and faithfully filled her with the power of the Spirit. Though I did not ask for any money, she said she wanted to bless me with a gift. She gave me five hundred dollars. With that, I would easily be able to buy the doll that Edilyn had wanted. My friends took me to the store, and to my joy, I found the doll.

As I checked in my luggage for the return trip, I did not have enough space to pack the doll. We were only allowed two carry-on items. I already had my purse and carry-on bag. The airport officer stopped me and said I could not take all three. I would have to choose two and leave the other behind. Since I needed the other things, I sadly left the doll behind. It broke my heart.

After I was seated aboard the plane, a man coming down the aisle motioned for me. He had a grin on his face. He held up the box that had my doll for Edilyn! He said he saw the sadness in my countenance when I had to leave the doll behind. Since he had no on board luggage, he asked to take the box as his carry-on. The airport security had no issues with his request. When I returned home, Edilyn was so happy with her gift. I thanked God for even the small things He blesses us with (James 1:17).

Glen and I filed for my green card and my eventual citizenship in the United States in early 1992. It was never my intention to remain in America, but to travel back and forth to continue the ministry. I would remain in my native country usually from three to six months at a time. I eventually petitioned for Edilyn and Christine to join us in the United States. Edilyn was fourteen and Christine was twelve when they finally arrived. I could not petition my sons because the Philippine law at that time stated that if you are over 16 years of age, it was not allowed. Bong and Jojo remained with family members in Davao City and eventually had families of their own.

◆◆◆

10

MINISTRY TO MUSLIMS

During one of the services at Trinity Chapel, a visiting minister prophesied over me and said that I would return to the Philippines and minister to a Muslim community. The thought of such a thing put fear into my heart, for I knew how fierce they could be. Many of them were not trustworthy. Though I had encountered Muslims before when ministering alongside Edith Watson, I would now be dealing with them directly. I pleaded with the Lord over these fears I had, but I felt like He was assuring me that His Presence would go with me.

When I returned to the Philippines, a Christian lady approached me and asked if I could be of help to the Islamic community. She lived with her family who were Muslims. She was burdened for the kids and young people because they were malnourished and sickly. She didn't want me to openly speak of the gospel, since the Imam of the local mosque was so strict. I prayed about her warning, for I really desired for God to do something in that place. I was willing to go, but I still felt uneasy about being among this type of community. I knew that some Christian missionaries had been killed while trying to minister among the Muslims.

The village we would be working in was under strict control. It was in Sasa near the seashore. The young Christian lady who asked me to help her had also asked some churches to help with this project, but they turned her down because they didn't have the funds or the availability to assist. I felt that this was the Lord's confirmation that I was to step in and work among them. I continued to battle with fear over the possible conflict with the Imam. I told the Lord that in spite of this, I would go forward because I knew He would watch over me.

The scene was a sad one. Many of the children were very hungry and fighting various illnesses. They swarmed us and seemed happy to see fresh, new faces in their midst. The people in that village told us that many of the kids were uneducated. At that particular time, there was no preschool in Sasa or in any part of Davao. After talking it over with my Christian friend, I felt the Lord was leading me to start a preschool for kids where we would sing songs and tell stories. We would do it in secret from the Islamic leaders. We had a small, secluded space where we fed the kids. This included candies the children loved. We secured tables and chairs to use. We taught the kids to write. We visited a nearby clinic to see if the medical staff could help these young ones. We continued feeding these hungry kids every day.

The parents were happy with our feeding program. One

mother even tried to give up her baby to us for adoption since she couldn't care for the child's needs properly, but our frequent travel made it impossible for us to do so. We arranged for another godly, loving couple to take the child.

Not long after this, we spread the word in the community that we were starting a preschool where children would receive food regularly along with some education. As we were enrolling children in the preschool, a Muslim father approached us, carrying his son in his arms. The child could not walk because of a condition that crippled him. The little boy was crying because he wanted to join the school. I asked how old he was, and the father told me the boy was seven years of age. I told the father we would be glad to have him join our school, but I would like to pray for him first. The father said we could do whatever we wanted as long as we agreed to admit his son into the school. After we prayed for the child, he wanted his father to put him down. For the first time in his life, the boy was able to walk! The father wanted to know who our God was, for the one he believed in could not do that. The mother and the rest of the family of this healed boy were excited with the news of this miracle. They invited other Muslim families to come with them and hear the gospel of Jesus Christ from our lips. That whole family became converts and asked to be baptized in water. The miracle boy has since grown up to be strong and healthy. We have sent support for him to go to school and get a good education. The healing of the crippled child was not only the catalyst to bring the gospel and baptism to his family; it drew others to hear the good news.

Even though some of them were open to receiving the good news of the gospel, there were others who would not be so willing. We continued to secretly teach them about being a

Christian. The Holy Spirit led another family to come forward seeking salvation and the healing of their paralyzed father. The Lord granted both requests. After we prayed for the head of this household, he was gloriously healed and the family became believers.

To keep our relationship with the Lord healthy, we often visited a prayer house on top of a mountain in the Toril community. It had been established by other missionaries who had gone before us. We would spend many nights there in prayer before the Lord. It refreshed and renewed our souls.

I made many trips back and forth between the Philippines and the United States. During one of those brief returns to America, a friend named Bill Andrews called me and asked when I would return to the mission field. He was an architect whom I had gotten acquainted with at our home church in Knoxville. I told Bill that I intended to go back quickly, but I had not yet purchased a plane ticket. He came to the house and provided the funds to pay for my travel back to the mission field. I ministered in the Philippines again for a few months and returned to the United States after another fruitful time among my people.

Before one of my trips back home, I had asked God to provide me with a van in the Philippines so that I could move around the region more effectively. While I was praying, an impression came to me that the Lord would provide a $10,000 check to fund my request. Filipino friends named Nelson and Beth, who were part of a Southern Baptist Bible Study group, asked me to join them and share my testimony about the ongoing work in the Philippines. I readily agreed. After I shared what was happening in the ministry, one of the men in the group named Jesse Morris said they normally do not receive an offering at these gatherings, but they were willing to do so now. He reached into his pocket and pulled out two hundred dollars and handed it to me. Jesse said it was odd because he never carries around pocket money like that. We all believed it was an appointment of God for this to happen so he could bless the Lord's work in the Philippines.

The biggest blessing of all was yet to come. A week later, Jesse wrote out a check and placed it in my hands. It was for $10,000! His wife Julias gave me an additional check to provide funds for my needs during the trip.

When I told Jesse about my prayer, he shared his testimony. He was originally from Germany. He was not wealthy, nor was he a minister, but he loved to go from house to house and distribute gospel tracts to people. One of Jesse's elderly neighbors fell ill. When Jesse found out, he visited with him. The old man had no family nearby. His closest relative was a sister living in New York. So Jesse cared for the sick man, taking him to doctor visits and checking in on him regularly. When the elderly neighbor was dying, Jesse found out that his neighbor had plenty of money, and gave it to Jesse in his will. Jesse's neighbor was supporting missionaries from other countries, and he wanted Jesse to continue giving to mission work. Jesse said he would only use the funds in the way he had promised. From that point on, Jesse Morris became a regular supporter of my ministry in the Philippines. How wonderful are the ways in which the Lord supplies our every need (Psalms 37:25).

I would continue to minister to the people in my homeland, but I had to do it alone at times. Glen had chronic heart issues which prevented him from traveling with me. Even though my husband was not always by my side, the Presence of the Lord was my constant companion. After twenty wonderful years of marriage to Glen, he passed into the Presence of Jesus.

Despite being widowed again, I continued to serve the Lord with the help and the strength of the Holy Spirit. I was not only experiencing Christ's resurrection power, but also the fellowship of His suffering (Philippians 3:10).

◆◆◆

11

DESPAIR AND THE DIVINE

When I returned to the Philippines to minister among the people of Davao City once again, I lived in the house of my second son Jojo. As you would suspect, many knew my ministry. One morning, the helper who stayed in his home knocked on the door of my room. I opened to see what she wanted. Tears streamed down her face. She was filled with despair. She told me that her brother, who was in another town, was digging in the gold mines and got injured when a large rock fell on top of him and crushed his stomach. The brother was rushed to the hospital. The body scans revealed that his liver had been smashed. The girl wanted to go visit her brother because he needed additional white blood cells to help his immune system fight the damage from the injury.

I was not feeling well at that time because I was battling the flu. Even though I was struggling with the symptoms of the flu, my heart was gushing with compassion. I told the helper that we would go together and see this brother and find some suitable blood for him.

In order to get the proper blood to the helper's brother, we would need to visit a blood bank and have money to buy it. I had my ATM card from my American bank, but I didn't have any funds in my account. I was thinking God would supply since this was an emergency, and perhaps something would be in there. We needed four thousand pesos for one bag of blood, so that is what I believed for. Sure enough, money came out. I had five thousand pesos. My friend Loretta Ehlers had put money into the account. She had been trying to call me and tell me that the Lord had spoken to her about adding some money into my account. God was on time with this need!

When we found a blood bank, there was a long line of people ahead of me. I was praying that we could move more quickly because I knew the need was desperate. The man at the desk in front of the line motioned for me. I was surprised and could not believe he was talking to me. I made my way up to his desk and he asked me what it was that I needed. I told him I had an emergency and I needed a bag of white blood cells. He told me he was sorry. They had run out. I began to silently pray again for the Lord to supply this need. I asked this man if he would check again, for I was sure he would have some in storage. I think he went to check on it just to humor me and keep me from harassing him. Sometimes persistence brings the needed answer just like in the parable Jesus told (Luke 18:1-8). The man came back with a strange look on his face. He found one bag of white blood cells.

It was all that I needed. The Lord had come through again, but He wasn't finished.

It took an hour and a half by bus to reach the hospital. By the time we arrived, it was already night. The security officer was unwilling to allow us to enter. Visiting hours were over. I was begging the guard to let us in. I explained the emergency we faced. I told him that I am a missionary who had come a long way to help. I told him that I wanted to lead a dying person to God so he could go to Heaven. The Lord moved the heart of this man, and he said he would give me a few minutes with the patient.

I entered the hospital and went to the ICU where this injured man was. The nurse met me and told me that I could not get in to see him. I would only be allowed to look through the window. I told her that I needed to talk to him about God. The Lord moved upon her heart as well. I was the only one permitted to see the injured man. As I stood over his bed, I noticed that his eyes were closed. Several tubes were in and around his body. I asked him if he could hear me. He nodded. I told him that I wanted him to know that Jesus loved him. If he was going to die, he could go to Heaven if he would accept Jesus as his Savior. I told him I did not have much time to visit, so I wanted to pray with him about accepting Jesus into his heart. He could not talk because of all the tubes in his mouth, so I told him to just pray silently in his heart. As I mouthed the words of prayer, I saw tears welling up in his eyes and streaming down his face.

The nurse started signaling for me to leave. I asked if I could have just a few more minutes to pray for this man's healing. I bowed over him and told him that he was ready for Heaven, but God could heal him from this injury. He started nodding again. I found out that he had a sweetheart, and they were planning to get married. I told him to just believe God for a miracle, and we prayed a simple prayer together. I did it out loud and he did it in his heart.

I met the family of the injured man outside. I stopped to talk with them and share the gospel. I told them about his conversion and about our prayer for his healing. The hearts of some of the family members began to melt, and they also prayed to believe in the Lord Jesus.

By the time I left the hospital, it was almost midnight. I rode on a small tricycle to the nearby bus station. When I arrived, there was no more transportation until the next day. The buses were no longer running. The tricycle was not made for such a long trip. I prayed that the Lord would supply the need. A taxi pulled up close to the bus station, a man got out and he stood outside his vehicle. I hurried over to him and asked if he was taking passengers. I told him I needed to go back to Davao City. He said it was not a problem. No one else was around that night, and he just happened to make a random, brief stop to relax. The Lord came through once again for His servant!

Several miracles happened on that night. That young man I prayed for eventually left the hospital, got married, and shared his testimony everywhere he went. Many people came to faith because of it. I would never forget what the Lord did, and I promised Him that I would also share His faithfulness wherever I went and whenever I had the opportunity (Psalms 145:5).

◆◆◆

12

BACK AND FORTH

I have a few more stories of the Lord's moving during my various trips to the Philippines. Here are some of them:

During one of my trips to the Philippines, I ministered to a Filipino lady who had been a nurse in New York. She had hurt her arm and decided to return to the Philippines. We met through a mutual friend named Linda Maci. Linda said that we needed to pray for the injured arm of her nurse friend. It had been fractured and had left her crippled. The nurse was not a believer at that time. We led her to the Lord and she started attending Bible studies. She asked for prayer all the time. One day Linda came to me and said her nurse friend wanted to be baptized in water like the Bible commands. We went to a swimming pool and performed the baptism according to the teaching. When she came up out of the water, she started praising God. Her crippled arm had been completely restored after coming up out of the waters.

On another occasion, the mother-in-law of my son Jojo was trying to witness to her relative's family about Jesus. The husband was paralyzed. She invited me to come and pray for the whole family in their home. I accepted the invitation. When we gathered together, I started reading the Bible and sang a short chorus. I prayed for the paralyzed man and the whole family was touched with the prayer and the sweet Presence of the Lord in our midst. After that, he felt something in his body and began to move. A few days later, I heard the man was continuing to improve. We later heard he was completely healed and went back to work. It just reminded me that God heals in His own way and in His own time!

While I ministered in the Philippines, I was asked to speak on a local radio program. I was not feeling well at the time and debated as to whether I should do it. The friend who had asked me prayed for me to feel better, so by faith I went. After I spoke on the radio, a man came to the station and asked if I would come to his church and talk about the Holy Spirit, for that was the subject I had talked about on air. It was a Catholic church that was interested in the power of the Spirit. It was a Pentecost Sunday celebration.

Their church was a large cathedral in Cotabato City. It is over four hours away from Davao City. I didn't tell them I was not Catholic. I sat up front on the first pew. I was the only woman there. The reason the leadership had asked me to speak about the Holy Spirit was because it was the Day of Pentecost, the seventh Sunday after Easter. After I talked about the power of the Holy Ghost, several people came forward to be baptized in the Spirit.

One day while riding on one of the buses, some people who had heard me speak at their church were riding too. They approached me and gave me money for transportation. I did not ask for it, but this kind of thing happened often without me saying a word about it. The Lord even meets my needs before I know I need it!

Sometimes the Holy Spirit worked through multiple circumstances to guard me and open other doors of opportunity. In May of the year 2000, I finished another time of ministry in the Philippines and prepared to come back to America. I was scheduled to depart on Thursday May 25, 2000. When I woke up early the morning before my departure, I had a strange feeling. I was weak in body and not up to leaving. I told my son, whom I was staying with, to cancel my trip. My son did as I had requested and he rescheduled the flight.

The next day, I heard news reports that the plane I was to board in Davao City had been hijacked. It was a flight from Davao City to Manila. Minutes before landing in the airport at Manila, the hijacker with a hand grenade and pistol, ordered the plane back to Davao City. The plane did not have enough fuel to make another 600-mile trip. He collected jewelry and money from the passengers in a bag. The hijacker then went to one of the exits wearing a parachute he invented. A flight attendant opened the exit after the plane slowed its speed and reduced its altitude. She had to push the man out of the plane. His homemade parachute failed and his dead body was found near Manila. The bag of loot was never found.

Later that same day, a friend called me and said she had been praying she could reach me. She wanted me to go to the hospital with her to pray for her father who was dying. She wanted her father to get saved before he passed away. I was allowed to go back into this man's room and pray for him. He was in a coma in the ICU. I shared the gospel with him regardless, hoping he could hear me. I took this man by the hand and asked him to squeeze my hand if he could hear me. I felt a quick squeeze. I prayed a prayer for salvation and asked him to follow along with me in his heart. He squeezed my hand again as the tears flowed from his eyes. I knew he had accepted Jesus into his heart. I was overjoyed that another sinner had been washed by the blood of the Lamb. I was told that the man died the following day. What a wonderful change of plans directed by our heavenly Father! He knows what is best for us. We only need to follow where He leads!

During another one of my brief mission trips, I had a church staff working with me for visitation to homes every other day in the church that God had used me to plant in Panacan near Davao City. We had opportunities for Bible study and exhortation in many homes. One of the families in the village invited us to hold a meeting in their house. They were new converts and had a teenage daughter who acted strangely. The parents said she had been sick with insomnia and mental problems. They sold a parcel of their land to get their daughter treatment, but there was no help for her. The ones who examined her said she was insane. She was dressed in tattered clothing. While I and my four companions were visiting, we watched this young girl jump and act weird. Before we began our Bible study, we prayed for this young lady. We started singing There is Power in the Blood. We sang that song over and over again.

As this teenage girl listened, she got up and started dancing to our voices. We did not let that stop us. We kept singing and worshiping Jesus. Eventually, the girl got tired of dancing. She dropped to the floor and fell asleep. As we finished our worship time and prepared to start the Bible study, the girl rose up and asked what we were doing. Her senses had returned to her. She wanted to change clothes and eat something. There had been a dramatic change in her demeanor as we sang about the blood of Christ. Every time we had the Bible study, she was eager to participate. What a great miracle by the hand of our great God!

During some of my mission endeavors, there are times when we were so busy in the work of the Lord that I grew very weary. We had Bible studies and other meetings every day. Sometimes we gathered in the morning, in the afternoon and in the evening. Though there was great joy in serving Jesus, it was especially wearisome when dealing with troubles and setbacks during our times of ministry. A couple from the church invited me into their home to get away and have a time of sabbatical. I took that opportunity to spend time in the Presence of the Lord and be refreshed by His Spirit. It also gave me the chance to hear clearly from God and discern where He was leading me next. I would often unwind and recover from extensive ministry outings in the Philippines when I returned to the United States. I knew it was important to have that balance in my life and calling, for even Jesus and His disciples took time to rest (Mark 6:31).

The Lord continued to provide for the ongoing ministry in the Philippines. As I pondered over these things, I received requests to minister in several towns and villages back home. The Lord was opening doors of opportunity upon my arrival. I just needed the supply to get there and fulfill the divine obligations. God never failed me in that. I would continue to travel from America to the Philippines on several mission trips. I would minister to the churches in Davao and encourage them to remain faithful to the work of God.

During one of my final mission trips to the Philippines, the Lord imparted prophetic words to me through members of my home church. On September 22, 2013, a fellow church member, Esther Heneise, had a vision during our international house church meeting. She wrote it down and I taped it to the back of my Bible. It says, "I saw two guardian angels, big and fiery. They had locked arms together and made a chair with their arms and you were sitting in the chair (their arms) and they were carrying you everywhere you went." On July 27, 2014, a vision came to Chris Harris, a fellow church member, during worship at church. He also wrote it down and I taped it in my Bible. It says, "I felt that when you were walking in this morning, I had a vision that you were walking in the footsteps of the Lord. He is strengthening you now even when you are feeling weak. When we are weak, God is strong." These words brought great encouragement to me and helped me to carry on during that particular trip. Though I was slowing down, the Lord was still powerfully doing His work through me.

Whether it was physical strength, financial offerings, spiritual deliverance or whatever the need, God always provided every good gift (Matthew 7:11). Praise His holy Name!

◆◆◆

13

PLANTED IN INTERCESSION

As I reflect back on my life and ministry, it is amazing at what the Lord had accomplished through me over the years as I yielded myself to Him. I know that nothing could have succeeded without the Presence and power of the Holy Spirit. Even as we put this book together, I had some difficulty remembering names, dates and the timing of the events that happened, but the Lord was faithful and brought to mind those things that He wanted me to share.

Since I have become older and all the health issues that come with age, I struggle with the fact that I cannot go for the Lord as I once did. My trips to the Philippines are hard to manage, though I do oversight my remaining ministry and keep in contact with many ministries in Davao. I continue to minister to my family and friends here in Knoxville, Tennessee. I look for simple ways in day to day routines to share Jesus with people. It can be as simple as the time I went into Wal-Mart and watched people hurriedly going in and out. I was praying for an opportunity to share my faith with someone. A woman caught my eye who looked so sad. I felt the Holy Spirit prompting me to tell her that God loved her. When I told the woman these words, her eyes lit up. She said no one had ever told her that, and she needed to hear it. She thought God was mad at her.

I try to send the Filipino missionaries support through the Balikbayan box (a specialized box filled with goods sent to the Philippines by boat or plane for one low price) and financial gifts. I ship books, clothing, food and other necessities. It is common for Filipinos to send money and goods to their families in the Philippines. In Tagalog, balikbayan means "back home". It refers to Filipinos returning to one's country. For many Filipinos living and working around the world, they eventually go back to the Philippines for good or for a visit.

There is still much work to be done, and I am happy to know God is raising up many others to carry on the work. The needs are endless, so the giving must be endless. I've learned over the years that the more obedient we are to the Lord, the more He will bless us and others. His grace, love and mercy know no bounds!

There are times I feel discouraged about my physical limitations. My hearing has deteriorated along with my vision. I have limited mobility and battle with bouts of weakness. It has become harder to be engaged in Bible studies and even day-to-day routines. I have often prayed that God would take me to Heaven, but I realize that He is not finished with me yet. I know that when I am weak, then the Lord is strong. Jesus works mightily within me and gives me strength to carry on.

I was reminded of this recently when I went to the hospital to have an endoscopy. My stomach had been hurting chronically and I got choked in my throat at times. The day of the procedure, I was nervous. I did not sleep at all the previous night. Many people prayed during my test. A lady from AGLOW (a charismatic women's group with a local chapter here in Knoxville, TN that I have been a part of) called me and said the Lord showed her that angels were with me during this. When I went to my appointment, the medical staff allowed my daughter Edilyn to come into the operating room with me because of my poor hearing. My heart was not feeling right when they tried to give me anesthesia, so they decided not to go through with it. I have had some relatives die during a similar test, but the Lord spared me. He wanted me to finish this book! I prayed the Lord would bring the healing to me He had given to so many others. My pain subsided at the hospital but does continue to flare up at times.

Moreover, I am continuously encouraged by Psalms 34. It is my favorite Scripture.

"I will bless the Lord at all times. His praise shall continuously be in my mouth My soul shall make her boast in the Lord: The humble shall hear thereof and be glad. O magnify the LORD with me, And let us exalt His Name together. I sought the LORD, and He heard me, And delivered me from all my fears. They looked to Him and were lightened: And their faces were not ashamed. This poor man cried, And the LORD heard him, And saved him out of all his troubles. The Angel of the LORD encampeth round about them that fear Him, And delivereth them .O taste and see that the LORD is good: Blessed is the man that trusteth in Him. O fear the LORD, ye His saints: For there is no want to them that fear Him.

The young lions do lack, and suffer hunger. But they that seek the LORD shall not want any good thing. Come ye children, hearken unto me: I will teach you the fear of the LORD. What man is he that desireth life, And loveth many days, that he may see good? Keep thy tongue from evil, And thy lips from speaking guile. Depart from evil, and do good; seek peace and pursue it. The eyes of the LORD are upon the righteous, And His ears are open to their cry. The face of the LORD is against them that do evil, To cut off the remembrance of them from the earth. The righteous cry, and the LORD heareth, And delivereth them out of all their troubles. The LORD is nigh unto them that are of a broken heart; And saveth such as be of a contrite spirit. Many are the afflictions of the righteous: But the LORD delivereth him out of them all. He keepeth all his bones: Not one of them is broken. Evil shall slay the wicked: And they that hate the righteous shall be desolate. The LORD redeemeth the soul of His servants: And none of them that trust in Him shall be desolate." (Psalms 34:1-22 KJV)

When I am troubled, I am encouraged by my favorite songs In the Garden and What A Friend We Have in Jesus. Those hymns comforted me on many occasions. In the times I felt alone, I would hum them to myself and suddenly sense the overwhelming, loving Presence of my sweet Savior:

Planted In Intercession

I come to the garden alone

While the dew is still on the roses

And the voice I hear falling on my ear

The Son of God discloses.

He speaks, and the sound of His voice,

Is so sweet the birds hush their singing,

And the melody that He gave to me

Within my heart is ringing.

I stayed in the garden with Him

Though the night oil around me be falling,

But He bids me go; through the voice of woe

His voice to me is calling.

And He walks with me, and He talks with me,

And He tells me I am His own;

And the joy we share as we tarry there,

None other has ever known.

Charles Austin Miles (1912

God's Faithful Ways

What a friend we have in Jesus,

All our sins and griefs to bear!

What a privilege to carry

Everything to God in prayer!

Oh, what peace we often forfeit,

Oh, what needless pain we bear,

All because we do not carry

Everything to God in prayer!

Have we trials and temptations?

Is there trouble anywhere?

We should never be discouraged—

Take it to the Lord in prayer.

Can we find a friend so faithful,

Who will all our sorrows share?

Jesus knows our every weakness;

Take it to the Lord in prayer.

Are we weak and heavy-laden,

Cumbered with a load of care?

Precious Savior, still our refuge—

Take it to the Lord in prayer.

Do thy friends despise, forsake thee?

Take it to the Lord in prayer!

In His arms He'll take and shield thee,

Thou wilt find a solace there.

Blessed Savior, Thou hast promised

Thou wilt all our burdens bear;

May we ever, Lord, be bringing

All to Thee in earnest prayer.

Soon in glory bright, unclouded,

There will be no need for prayer—

Rapture, praise, and endless worship

Will be our sweet portion there.

Charles C. Converse (1868)

I have recently been seeing heavenly visions of my loved ones. I know God is giving me a sneak peek into what lies ahead for me. They are arrayed in white robes. I am getting so excited to see them in our eternal home!

On May 1st of 2024, I ended up in the hospital with an irregular heart rhythm and a severe cough from a virus I had contracted. I endured several days of poking and prodding from needles and tubes. It was so uncomfortable, just lying there day after day. I wanted to give up and let the Lord take me to Heaven, but many people were praying for my healing. While I was in and out of sleep, I could hear the angels singing to me. They were singing songs such as Great Is Thy Faithfulness and What A Day That Will Be. It gave me new encouragement to get better and keep going for the Lord. I was finally discharged after a week, fully recovered. God saw to it that I get well so the book could be finalized!

It has taken nearly four years for this manuscript to be finished. I can finally say, by the grace of God, I have fulfilled what the Spirit put in my heart. As long as I have breath in my body, I will continue to serve Jesus for His honor and glory. The time of the end is coming soon, and we need to be ready to go to Heaven. On that note, I have one more thing to add.

◆◆◆

14

A FINAL PLEA TO ALL

The purpose of this book is to help us not only feed our faith occasionally, but every single moment of every single day. I hope it has shown us how faithful the Lord is and that it has encouraged us to keep going until we develop the kind of mountain moving faith that will make us more than a conqueror in every area of life.

In Mark 11:23, we see that God works in mysterious ways; His wonders and miracles He will perform in these end times, for His glory and honor. Before and after my graduation from Bible school, I had such a great desire to follow the Lord and serve Him. I stepped out in faith to follow the Great Commission of Jesus to His disciples.

The gospel of Christ is the main reason we have produced this book. It shows us what God has done. In Romans 1:16 and Matthew 24:14, we see that the gospel of the kingdom should be preached to all nations. Isaiah 52:7 shows us how God described those that preach the gospel, the good news of God's story. In 2 Timothy 4:2, we see that we are to preach His words to others, which is sharing our faith. God equips us with power as we bring the gospel. (Luke 24:49) The result of preaching the gospel is found in Acts 4:4 and Acts 6:7. God promised us that if we obey the Lord and follow Him by taking the gospel to people around us and to all nations, then there is victory for the faithful ones. (Psalms 126:6)

Ever since sin entered the human experience (Genesis 3:1-19), we have been estranged from our Father in Heaven and from our eternal, true home. This is the reason that we all need Christ. Our heavenly Father sent Jesus His Son into the world to provide a way back to God. Jesus lived a perfect life. Then He took our place and bore our punishment as a sacrifice for our unrighteousness and disobedience against God. Christ's death dealt with our sin and became the very thing that made our return to God now possible. Paul the apostle explains it this way. Christ died for our sins according to the scriptures. He was buried and He was raised on the third day according to the scriptures. (1 Corinthians 15:3-4)

This is good news because of God's amazing love! He was willing to pay that ultimate price to bring us home. Scripture reveals we just need to simply accept this free gift of forgiveness and restoration to receive salvation and eternal life. So if we declare with our mouth Jesus is Lord, and believe in our heart that God raised Him from the dead, we will be saved. (Romans

10:9) God offers us an invitation to come to Him, both now and forever. Only one question remains. Will you accept this amazing gift by faith? For those who read this book and are not sure of your salvation, making a decision to believe in Him is the first step. Following Jesus thereafter is what proves you have truly surrendered your heart to Him. You are not saved by your good works, but they are the evidence that God has really changed your life and you will enjoy the rewards in Heaven waiting for you as you remain faithful to God!

The story of the prodigal son illustrates a turning point. The son took the inheritance of his father's wealth and squandered it on just about every indecency possible. Distress paid him a visit. When he had spent everything, a severe famine occurred in that country. He became impoverished. He would gladly fill his stomach with the bad food that the swine were eating (Luke 15:14-16). Disgusting? Yes. But that is what awaits anyone on the road of "doing my own way."

Now you must decide if it will be your way or God's way. It is a choice you must make. Accepting Jesus into your life is not just a religious act that you perform to get to Heaven, but it is an experience that you must have that changes the heart and makes life fulfilling. There is an emptiness in everyone's heart that only God can fill. Notice what the prodigal son did. He came to his senses. He got up and came back to his father. (Luke 15:17-20) We can clearly see that his decision prompted him to action. That is what true faith looks like. What did his father do? He saw the wayward son and felt compassion for him. That is what God does when we come to Him. He opens His arms wide to receive us. No matter who you are or what you've done. God sees you and loves you so much. He wants to fulfill His wonderful plan in your life.

For those who are backslidden and have gone away from God after experiencing His redemption, repent and come back to the Lord to receive His forgiveness. Let Him once again rule in your heart as you did when you first accepted Christ into your life. As many as received Him, to them gave He power to become the sons of God. (John 1:12) This includes all who are called according to His purpose. That is God's promise to His people. Commit your life to the Lord and live close to Him. Read your Bible. Pray and share your experience. Jesus is the way, the truth and the life. There is no peace, no joy and no satisfaction outside of Christ. He is the answer to all our needs.

I thank God that I have had the privilege to witness the mighty power of God in my lifetime. Since I have accepted Christ as my Savior, I didn't want to just know Him in my head, but know Him in my heart and have a personal relationship with Him. It is an intimate friendship where we can see God move in abundance of life that is available to His people. I praise God for this opportunity to bring these things to print. I also thank Him for sending people to help me produce it. Before I end, I will say a prayer for everyone who is reading this:

Father God,

How thankful and grateful we are to know You Lord, that even though this world has fallen through the sin of Adam and Eve and made us all sinners who come short of Your glory, we can come to You Father God, through Your Son Jesus Whom You sent to suffer, to die and Who was resurrected on the third day. You completed our salvation and redeemed us from our sin.

We praise You, Lord God, for what You have been doing.

What You have done before, You are still doing now and more. You are the same yesterday, today and forever. I am praying, O God, for all those that read this book, that You will touch their hearts. I pray that they will not only read and enjoy it, but that those things I spoke of, that they think might be too good to be true, would come to realize that it is all true because Jesus is truth. It is You Lord that did a work in my own life. You wanted me to share this testimony with everyone.

So, I will keep on praising You Lord. It is not because of me that these wonderful things took place, but it's all because of You using me as Your instrument. I pray that everyone who reads this book will be challenged, O God, to have the love and desire to serve You in every way that You lead them. Thank You for blessing all Your people. We claim more souls for Your kingdom as they read about these marvelous stories of Your glorious power. I ask for a special blessing upon all in the mighty Name of Jesus. Amen and amen!

◆◆◆

The following is a series of appendices which provide additional news and recount the experiences of Ninfa Parsons during visits to the Philippines. It also covers events connected to Ninfa's ministry partners. These reports reveal God's hand in her life and show the ongoing fruitfulness of her labors.

APPENDIX A

MINISTRY NEWSLETTER
(MISSION FROM APRIL TO JUNE 1993)

Dear praying friends,

The Lord girded me with strength (Psalms 18:39).

Upon coming home to my own people, I was swamped with a lot of needs and problems. Our concerns are also the Philippine government's daily battles...power problems, shaky economy, poverty, rampant crimes and others. The people are getting used to them. The conditions of even the church workers and pastors are not encouraging.

On May 31st, the Lord gave me a word, that God the Holy

Spirit was moving in "lightning effects," and that I'd feel the quickness of the Lord's hand as I journey even to "new" places. Hallelujah! I was literally girded with new strength. The Lord proved His Word.

Since I arrived last April 8th, the Lord opened doors for me to speak and minister in new places, to new groups, to different people, and of course to a few familiar groups too. I have seen the Lord move in a glorious way. The anointing of the Lord is so strong; people are coming to Jesus in repentance and committing their needs and problems to God. Many lives were touched and changed. There is great joy on their faces.

Last May 28th, I spoke and ministered to a family camp at the Temple of Praise Church. The parents and children were filled to overflowing with the Holy Spirit. There was a restoration of relationships.

Early the next day, I rushed by bus to another city to speak and minister to a joint ministers' fellowship from different denominations. At six in the evening, I ministered to a ladies' group in one of the churches. The following day, (which was Sunday morning) I ministered to another church in that city. After the service, I hurriedly took another bus back to Davao City for another meeting.

On June 4th, I found myself ministering to three groups on the same day and in the same place. This was the start of when I found myself ministering with unusual circumstances. There was no previous commitment, no plans, no prepared schedule or itinerary. A casual visitation to a pastor friend led to an immediate family gathering of eight pastors for one day, with me as their speaker. This was in "Hope Mountain," a hilltop retreat center in

Ulas, Davao City. In a nearby building, I also ministered to twenty young people. I alternated between two groups at the same time, while a third group of young people arrived later. As the Word of the Lord was ministered to them, it was followed by the laying on of hands. Many of them were slain in the Spirit. Glory to God!

During the June 6th Sunday worship service, eight military men were slain in the Spirit during the ministry time as the Word of God went forth. The rest of the congregation followed as the Holy Spirit's anointing poured out upon them.

Thank you for your prayers and your support. If not for that, I probably would not have mustered enough strength for the Saturday and Sunday ministry speaking engagements. Sometimes I spoke twice on Sunday, along with three or four times more during the week.

I pray the Lord will return what you've shared with me in manifold blessings.

Please pray with me for the revival of God's people and that He will give me the words to minister to needy souls in other places. The Lord richly bless you.

In His Love and Service,

Ninfa Parsons

♦♦♦

APPENDIX B

MINISTRY NEWSLETTER
MAY 2ND, 1995

Dear Partners,

Greetings in the most powerful and precious Name of Jesus!

We are writing you with great excitement in our hearts about the things God is doing in our lives, in our churches and in all nations of the world. The Spirit of the Lord is mightily moving everywhere, doing signs, wonders, and miracles, and drawing more people closer to God. Surely we are living in the end times, the most glorious and wonderful time of all ages, because it is ushering in the coming of our King of kings and Lord of lords! There will be no more problems, heartaches, sickness, tears and disappointments. We who are prepared and doing the will of God will be with Him forever in glory!

We praise God for what He is doing with the ministry in the Philippines. We can only show you some remarkable experiences in pictures, but everything that has been done has been preserved in the very heart of God. He alone knows what happens to a person that responds to His great love, and He alone is worthy to receive praise, honor and glory for the things He has done.

Praise God, you and I have been a part of these wonderful works because of our willingness and obedience. The task is not finished yet. We have to move on with God. There are great things ahead He wants to do through us. Let us continue to be willing and obedient so we can eat the good of the land (Isaiah 1:19). We want to see our nation and other nations of the world blessed and prosperous.

God is sending me back to the Philippines on the 27th of May. I may remain there for three to seven months. It will depend on the leading of the Lord once I get there. There is so much need and we believe God will provide. Glen may follow me if I have to stay longer. We need a house and a place to minister. We are helping pastors and workers, providing good study materials for their ministries. We also minister to them personally. We will go to different places like towns and villages to proclaim salvation, healing and deliverance.

We are sharing our heart's desire and eagerness to serve the Lord because we need your prayers and financial support. This would be your great opportunity to win and bless souls for the glory of God! The Philippines is a ripe harvest field. People everywhere from all walks of life are starving for God.

We appreciate and thank the Lord for whatever help you can extend to us. Be assured that we will remember you in our prayers for a hundred-fold return in blessings that the Lord has promised to those who invest in His kingdom work.

We love you. The Lord bless you and keep you!

Glen and Ninfa Parsons

◆◆◆

APPENDIX C

PRAISE REPORT FROM PHILIPPINE
MISSIONS BY NINFA PARSONS (FALL 1997)

We cannot help but share our Lord God's
Goodness

Psalm 107:9

Last July 8, 1997, four dear sisters in the Lord sought me to pray with them. We went to a beach and communed with God the whole day with our praises and adoration. The Lord impressed upon Cora, our precious sister in the Lord, that we start first with true repentance of our sins and forgiveness for one another before God. We had such a refreshing time that we resolved in our hearts to walk with God on a daily basis like Enoch did in Genesis 5:24. We went to Shrine Park consequently and carried out an intercession for friends and loved ones.

As we reflected, the Lord had impressed upon our hearts to do something for the weary of souls - to share a place of prayer - and help them carry on with the Lord. God gave us Cherith Home as a result. For a start, we have acquired two bookcases that will contain precious reading materials and Christian audio/video tapes to equip seekers and workers of the Lord and also for assisting in the replenishment of strength for their souls. This is our Lord's goodness as found in Psalm 107:9. He wants to equip through us.

Thank you for praying and sharing. You are very much a part of what God is doing in these last days.

In Christ's Love and Service,

Ninfa Parsons

♦♦♦

APPENDIX D

PRAISE REPORT FROM PHILIPPINE MISSIONS BY NINFA PARSONS

(SEPTEMBER 22ND, 2009)

Let us always bless the Lord at all times! His praise shall continually be in our mouth. O magnify the Lord, and let us exalt His Name together. Then we can shout to the world - "O taste and see that the Lord is good. Blessed is the man that trusts in Him." (Psalms 34)

Last May 2008, I was in the Philippines to continue the ministry God started in Panacan village. This is not too far from the city of Davao. Close to Panacan is where we have the preschool in the Muslim community.

The first structure we built in Panacan village was the Prayer House. Last year, we finished the building and made a library. The Lord provided money to finish the church. These are simple buildings with materials made from coconut tree lumber and bamboo. The foundation, such as the posts, flooring, and part of the walls, are cement. These things kept me very busy during my year-long stay. I also minister to people through Bible studies, speaking in churches, and participating in prayer groups. Last March, we had VBS for 200 children in our unfinished church. The

Lord confirmed His Word with signs, wonders, and miracles. Souls are hungry for God. They are getting saved and delivered. That is the reason for all the buildings God wanted us to erect. People in that village and the Muslim community are so happy that we have a gathering place to worship and grow in God and His Word. By faith, the church will be finished this year, along with all the other needs such as the sound system, chairs, musical instruments, etc. By faith, many more souls will be saved. I know God will provide because time is short. We are living in dangerous and critical times. But for God's people, it is the most exciting and glorious end-time move of God. I praise and thank God for giving me strength and grace to go on and do His mandate at 69 years of age.

If you desire to be a part of this great end time harvest of souls and the abundant flow of His blessings, you may send an email, contact Trinity Chapel or send a personal check to my daughter Edilyn Hall. You can also contact her by phone. It will get to me fast through my ATM in the Philippines. Just do as God leads you. Thank you so much for your love, prayers and support. May God bless you richly. My scheduled trip back to the Philippines is September 28th, 2009.

In God's Victorious Army,

Ninfa P. Parsons

◆◆◆

APPENDIX E

FOUR TESTIMONIES FROM THE PHILIPPINE ISLANDS (DECEMBER 12TH 2012 REPORT)

Testimony 1

There is a great revival going on right now in the Philippines. Young people are being used by the Lord in a mighty way. They always gather together to worship God. They hear His words being taught, preached, and prophesied. They pull down strongholds in spiritual warfare. They see visions and watch God perform signs, wonders, and miracles.

Those young people, after spending hours in prayer, went out to the streets to give out tracts and witness to people. They stopped by the funeral home afterward to view the body of the deceased grandmother they had been acquainted with. They were not allowed to enter the morgue because the mortician was planning to embalm her. They prayed God would send the guy out of the room so they could see her once more. Sure enough, the man went out to get something. The young people rushed into the room and laid their hands directly on the grandmother.

Suddenly, they watched as her body began to move. She started breathing. While praying they saw a vision of the woman's spirit trying to enter back into her physical body. She thanked the teens for their intercession but asked the youth not to pray for her return and just let her go. She told them she could not do much and just wanted to rest. She liked where she had been. It was an awesome and wonderful place. The young people stood in awe and worshiped God for the miracle. They watched as the woman passed on again with a smile on her face. Glory to God!

More young people are getting saved every day. Homosexuals are getting saved and delivered. Lives are being transformed!

Testimony 2

God is also using little children. Kids from seven to twelve years of age are having their own church. They gather to worship for hours at a time. They also preach and read the Bible. The Spirit of the Lord is moving in their midst. They speak in tongues and some are slain in the spirit. They go out to the hospitals and pray for the sick. Many believe them and receive the Lord. They, of course, have older ones with them to help and guide them.

On one of their hospital visits, they went through the children's ward where many beds were lined up with their sick peers. The anointed kids prayed over every one of the sick before they left. The young evangelists told the sick children that some of them would go home tomorrow because God will heal them.

The next day, the church children went back to the hospital and found that most of them had gone home! Only a few sick kids remained. The fiery children prayed again over the ones who were left and told them they too would go home the next day. Sure enough, the ward emptied! The children's church had proclaimed that they wanted to see the hospital empty. God is a miracle working God!

Testimony 3

Gi-An Pizzaro (Davao City, Philippines)

When Gi-An was still in her mother's womb, her mother planned to give her away instead of aborting her. The reason was poverty, for they could not properly provide for the child. They already had six children. Her husband had no job. Gi-An's mother cleaned houses and did laundry work for people with no income to spare. It wasn't enough to support her family properly.

My heart went out to her, but I was getting ready to leave for America. I gave some money to my sister and asked her to pay for the hospital delivery. One day, I received a call from my sister. She informed me that the Gi-An had come into the world, but had an infection of the blood and was dying. I sent more money for doctors and medicines. They did not have enough to cover that level of care. They were waiting for Gi-An to die. Of course, I was praying for God's intervention.

A few days later, I received another phone call. Thanks poured through the phone. It was the mother telling me that the baby was getting well. Since I could not take Gi-An with me, my brother and his family adopted her. She is now eight years old, completely healthy, doing well in school, and attends church with her godly family. Indeed Gi-An is a joy to everyone! Glory to God!

Testimony 4

A local evangelist was led by the Spirit to hold a crusade close to a town where war broke out. He was warned by many people not to do it because grenades were being thrown everywhere.

The Lord told the evangelist to go on and not to fear. God would be present to perform miracles. On the first night of the meeting, the Lord moved and many souls came forward for salvation and healing. When the gathering dispersed, the minister and the workers found some grenades under the seats where some of the people had sat, but none of them had exploded! The crusade continued the next day. This time, grenades were thrown and there was an explosion. Some people got hurt and rushed to the hospital. The evangelist and some of his co-workers visited and prayed for the victims. They also went to the wing where dead ones were being kept and began to pray. A great commotion stirred in the hospital because some of the dead bodies came back to life! There was great rejoicing for all that God had done and is still doing to this day. Praise the Lord!

Ninfa P. Parsons

◆◆◆

APPENDIX F

NEWS ARTICLE ABOUT NINFA PARSONS' MINISTRY

(AUTUMN, 2014)

Ninfa Parsons has been an instrument of God most of her life. As a native of the Philippines, she began ministering to Muslim people in her country at the age of 20. Now at 75, she continues to go strong.

Parsons recently returned from her latest trip to the small town of Panacan in Davao City in the southern part of the Philippines. She spoke to Powell Aglow members last week during a gathering at the home of her daughter, Edilyn Hall.

"There is so much bad news, chaos, natural disasters and fear going on in the world today," said Parsons. "The good news is God is in charge."

Parsons makes at least one trip per year to continue ministering to poor Muslims in her home country. She started Bible study groups, home prayer groups and pioneered some churches. She participates in senior and youth retreats and often makes sure the hungry are fed. She has seen many healed from disabilities and disease and has shared the gospel wherever she travels.

"Her faith is really awesome," said Hall. "Her ministry has built her faith."

Parsons is a member at Trinity Chapel in Knoxville. She is able to sustain her ministry to the Philippines thanks to financial support from church members and private individuals with a heart to see the lost converted to Christianity.

Parsons' message was one of encouragement and faith.

"God is still moving by His Spirit, manifesting Himself to those that seek and follow Him."

Parsons plans to return to the Philippines in December. She, her daughter and members of Aglow prepared traditional Philippine food for the group meeting.

"Her life and ministry is truly inspiring," said Aglow leader Diane Shelby. Aglow members meet each fourth Tuesday for worship.

Cindy Taylor

♦♦♦

APPENDIX G

A MINISTRY LETTER TO NINFA
(SPRING 2021)

I was in Davao City in April 2021 and visited the church we were supporting in Cotabato City. The name of the church is Jesus Christ, The Living Spring of Life. The church has grown large. They started seven additional churches in the villages. The names of the tribes included in this are Midsayap – twenty families, Dado – twenty families, Magno – forty families, Baka – thirty five families which include one hundred children, Tenoreo – building still under construction with numbers pending, Patil – under construction and a small church coming out from Davao, Nuro – working with the Opi. It is all orchestrated by God. I thank Him that I am privileged to be a part of this mission. Because of your teaching and ministry to me, I learned to serve God and be happy in doing it. All glory to Jesus! God works in mysterious ways, His wonders to perform! I hope to hear from you.

Cora Hansen

◆◆◆

Left: My first taste of ministry was with the Four Square Church with these young ladies.

Middle: The 13th Annual National Convention of the Foursquare Gospel Churches in the Philippines, March 3-7, 1971.

Bottom: Missionary Team

Children are drawn to the Lord by our giving of gifts. The library has served as a great gift to answer the hunger of many young believers.

Teaching people how to live for Christ is the heart of ministry.

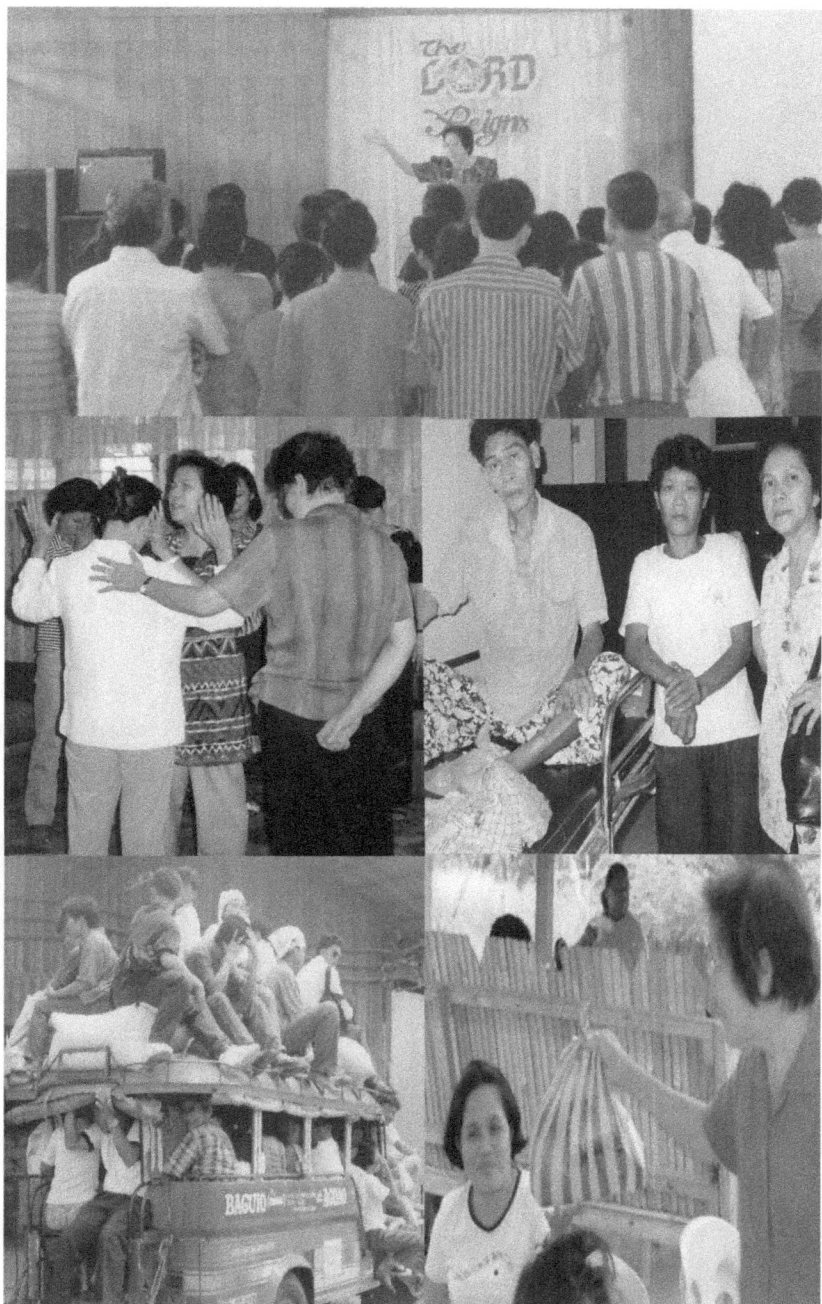

Whether we teach, comfort the sick, pray, take people to an event, or give goody bags, we offer the love of Christ.

www.ingramcontent.com/pod-product-compliance
Lightning Source LLC
Chambersburg PA
CBHW060117050426
42448CB00010B/1906